Art Cry

Memoirs of a Mural Painter

Patricia Ann Solveson

ArtCry Copyright © 2018 Patricia A. Solveson
All Rights reserved.

Independently published by the author
Patricia Ann Solveson
W7573 Rappy Lake Road Spooner,
Wisconsin 54801

ISBN 978-1-7324113-0-2

www.jerusalemwalloflife.org
First Printed in Jerusalem,
Israel Yanetz Printing Co.
Talpiot Jerusalem.

Art Cry

Memoirs of a Mural Painter

Contents

DEDICATION

This book of memoirs is dedicated to my husband, Carl Solveson. Carl has managed to overcome every obstacle imaginable to be able to love me for who I am. I only hope I have done the same for him. What are the odds of a Marine, a Vietnam Veteran no less, and a wild hippie girl making it together? Yet we have experienced tried and true love on our incredible journey. Without Carl's constant encouragement this book would have been impossible, but not only the book—my life would have had no possibility of succeeding without his quiet strength and the kind of love that says, "Honey, you can do this."

"To you, my darling Carl, I dedicate this book."

FOREWORD

It is always a privilege and a gift when someone is willing to share with us their personal journey. And Patricia's story is an incredible journey, as you will see! In the backwoods of northern Wisconsin, she overcame the impact of her perilous past during the cultural revolution of the 60's and 70's. Her ultimate destination however, was in the heart of Jerusalem, Israel, where she accomplished her life's work. For seven years Patricia poured out her art, painting an epic sized mural artistically illustrating the Bible.

It was not a simple task. It was always amazing to see Patricia painting and creating on this wall standing outdoors on scaffolding as the detailed and wonderful Biblical scenarios unfolded before our eyes. There were battles and victories, hardships and miracles, all of which Patricia so beautifully shares with us as this amazing work progressed.

You will truly be blessed as you share this journey with her through the pages of this book!

Esther Korson
Author of "I Am My Beloved's"
www.estherkorson.com

INTRODUCTION

Simply put, ArtCry is a news flash. In the excessive verbiage of the information age, ArtCry is an exclamation point that challenges you to pay attention to the direction our world is taking. ArtCry contains raw footage of the life of a woman who learned what not to do the hard way. It is a provocative story addressed to not only baby boomers, my contemporaries, but also to those in the church world who have drifted into religion instead of true spirituality that transforms human hearts. And most importantly, unlike fictional best sellers, this story is true. If you sense a strand of audacity, it is a slight hard edge on my heart from experiencing a world that I was completely unprepared to live in. There is also a touch of indignation that, all along the way, not one person possessed enough passion to warn me. I have emerged from this tunnel with power—the power of finding truth, though it came with a price tag. There are certainly no regrets that I paid the price, yet I would have regrets if my own passion was not enough to tell others.

When words are not heard, whether spoken or written, it does not matter; there is only one other means of direct communication that is compelling, in my opinion. This communication is through art—pictures that talk, paintings that move, though they are still. Painting has and always will be an opportunity for the daring to pour out their souls to a world that refuses to listen. May the beauty of art and a story now told, sweep you into a vista of greater altitudes which in turn redirect your pursuit of truth—liberating, beautiful, and dangerous truth.

PREFACE

Why not tell my story? I get a flutter of vulnerability when I think of telling all, but why not? There is no one else who has my exact story, no one else who has sung my song, and no one else who has painted my pictures. When I decided to write my memoirs, the go-ahead decision was rooted in one thing: could there be people or even just one person out there in this present scary world who would see something greater through my perspective? Or, perhaps glean enough hope to keep looking, keep searching, and ultimately find the treasure? No one else has spoken of these important life issues in the exact words that I use. Could it be that my way of expressing what happened to me, might strike a match for someone wandering in the dark? Let it be so!

Before you step into the flow of this book, there is something I need to articulate straight from my heart: God's love is for every person on the face of the earth. His passionate love is for everyone, every tongue and every tribe. Although I was invited to pour out my art on the Jewish side of the city, I discovered another group of people who also won my heart: the Arab Christians! I learned about the courage and fortitude of these believers whose challenges have escaped the awareness of many. I found precious friends among the Arabs whom I will always cherish, who helped me understand more fully God's love story for all people. It is so important to me that you know, this great love that can come only from God radiates in all directions.

Now the stage is set, wrapped in love and hopefully a lot of curiosity. May this book, birthed in pain, delivered with joy, hold something very special just for you.

Patricia Ann Solveson

PROLOGUE

"You have potential," said the psychic seated in front of me. Leaning forward on the edge of the daffodil print sofa in the fading light of early evening, in the home of this well-known psychic reader, an electric charge shot through my body. *"Really?"* This was an exciting thought for one who felt extremely insignificant. But more than feeling non-essential, at 23 years of age, I was terrified of life itself. I had no direction, only fears and worries of all kinds. What was in store for me? This is the haunting question that led me to make the first appointment with Claudia Garland, a well-known psychic in our state capital of Madison, Wisconsin. My friends, Mike and Pam Simmons, had already been to see her and had returned with an intriguing report. This mysterious woman called herself a psychometrist. She would hold a personal object such as a wristwatch and give a psychic reading that included information about the person's traits and their future. Pam said that she described their marriage to a T! Mike and Pam's marriage was falling apart and they were grasping at straws. They both had indulged in extramarital lovers and the damage was evident. This was my third visit to Claudia in two months. I was getting to know her a little more now. She had exciting stories of how her powers were used in the lives of even high level politicians in the capital city. She would tell stories about her enemies as well. These were the witches and warlocks of the city. But she proudly claimed that her power was white and used exclusively for good, even though there was a rumor that her powers had been solicited and then complicit in the death of a powerful city official. No one officially accused her. But it seemed to be veiled evidence that she was respected in all the levels of the psychic underworld.

Claudia continued with her remarks about me: "Yes, I am getting a strong impression that you have a rare sensitivity in the psychic realm. With a little tutoring you can develop this gift and help a lot of people in their lives."

It would be nice if I could do something worthwhile with my life; something, that is, besides working in a home for crazy kids, referring to my job with emotionally disturbed youths. My thoughts were racing now, a hook dangling in front of me with a tempting, juicy piece of prominence. "I would be willing to take you under my wing if you wish. This is an offer I do not give lightly. But I think my instincts about you are accurate." "I'd love nothing better" were the words that flew out of my mouth. I felt like I shouted it, but my voice was quiet in reality.

"Why don't you return next Thursday and we can begin. Would 1:30 p.m. work?"

CHAPTER I

Baby Boomers Forever

My involvement with the psychic woman marked the beginning of my slow plummet into a dark and mysterious world of supernatural and occult powers. You have heard the expression that ignorance is bliss! In my case, ignorance was not bliss, nor did it protect me from a cruel lesson that nearly cost me my life. What was it that compelled me to go in this direction? I was not alone in this ethereal pursuit. Hippies, by definition, delved into societal taboos without hesitation.

The post-World War II population explosion from 1946 through 1964 is known as the baby boomer generation. There are some unique characteristics of this group that I can personally attest to since I am part of it. The cultural changes experienced by baby boomers is not simple nor easy to comprehend. After World War II, the formalization of social units, whether family, religion, or school, had positive aspects as the population and the government grew, but there were also negative impacts. There developed a rigid social expectation; people who did not fit into the emerging institutionalized culture were rejected or ostracized. While high moral standards and personal integrity were idealized, most did not live up to this level and there developed among the baby boomer generation a sense that *all was not as it appeared.* Disillusionment took hold of many in my generation who experienced this hypocrisy. It came in many forms; some came through abuse of authority in one form or another. Some came when the government began to encroach into the lives of citizens in an unwanted manner. The Vietnam War came, and along with it, the draft.

From the aggregate of boomers, there were many who called themselves hippies. For better or for worse, the hippie population brought on changes in normative values, swayed politics, created pop culture, and defied mainstream society in general. Dubbed the 'Me generation,' our population group embellished the concept of self-fulfillment and gave it precedence over social responsibility. The goal of self-fulfillment was pursued by drug experimentation, sex apart from morality, and abandonment of what had become institutionalized Christianity, yet investigation into every other kind of religion, even supernatural occult activity.

My generation rebelled against the hypocrisy and the continual double standards imposed by those in authority. We felt justified in our defiance of social and moral rules. My own upbringing, unfortunately, played right into the hands of my rebellion through strict adherence to religious codes that took priority over nurturance, and which left no room for flexibility or personal freedom.

Visiting with Claudia became an obsession. I would drive to Madison, sometimes with my live-in boyfriend, Carl (who later became my husband), or several friends. We would receive psychic readings, give her some money, and make an appointment for the next time. She continued to tell me I had much potential as a psychic reader and give me pointers on how to receive psychic impressions. As I opened myself to this mindset, I began to receive impressions in my mind that did not seem to be coming from my natural intuition or my own thoughts.

There were times that I had what I called a 'premonition' that danger could be lurking on a certain highway, so I would alter my route. I would hear a phone ringing in my mind and then receive a phone call. It was uncanny. This happened repeatedly. Though minor instances, these were reinforcing the idea that I possessed psychic powers. In the apartment I shared with two young women, I began to hear sounds of someone coming up the six steps of our apartment entrance, yet there would be no one there. One day as I was sitting in my living room I felt someone enter the room. In fact, I saw someone enter the room in my peripheral vision, yet when I looked up I would see no one. After a few times, I kept my eyes down and was able to see a young man enter the room. I thought I even heard him speaking to me. It frightened me but I also knew that many people with psychic or mind powers also saw 'beyond the veil.' Later, in a different apartment, I began to see a little girl out of the 'corner of my eye.' This happened repeatedly. Years later I understood that I had allowed my soul to receive powers that would open what is known in the occult as the 'third eye.' This is the power that connects spirit and soul to be able to see into the spirit world. I learned later that the people I had been seeing were actually familiar spirits—spirits who came through family lines and manifested in the form of that deceased person. People in the New Age occult claim they are seeing the spirits of those departed through death. This is not true, however, it is all a part of the bigger deception that takes the blind on dangerous paths of the supernatural.

I was enthralled with the supernatural. So were many in the baby boomer generation. It seemed to come with the counter culture experimentation that captured so many young people. Drugs, sex, New Age, and occult all seemed to be part of the experience of the day. Wisconsin State

University began to sponsor psychic world conferences in their auditoriums. Workshops on spirit guides, automatic writing, eastern mysticism, visualization, shamanism, auras, chakras, psychic healing, Kirlian photography, and a host of new buzzwords were all set to thrill the New Age seekers.

With each new experience, I would crave more. Everything seemed alive and exciting. As an emerging adult, the freedom to make my own decision was intoxicating. I did not give much thought to whether my choices were wise or not. I wanted my independence and I grabbed it with gusto. My bruised and overly sensitive soul was toughened as I constructed inner walls to protect me from pain and anxiety that came from deep within. I hardened my heart to others and became stubborn and rebellious. I swore like a sailor, drank, and eventually took drugs.

In this adventurous independence I chose to go deeper into occult phenomena. My visits with Claudia became more frequent. I took the role of the mentored and she the mentor. There were times I worried whether or not I was into something dark and dangerous. When I questioned the validity of her craft, I would rationalize by reminding myself that she was a good Catholic and went to Mass frequently. Did not the Catholics have the one true church as I was taught in parochial school? Claudia would stay in the church after Mass to meditate and would always see things that no one else could see. She reported apparitions of angels and saints and various lights. I recall being with her at her church and straining to see what she saw. I lied when she asked me if I saw the same images that she saw. I said yes instead of admitting I saw nothing but a lot of bricks and a few statues and candles. The idea that she was somehow safe because she was a practicing Catholic gave me false confidence. This was ironic since I had rejected all forms of organized religion as did all bona fide hippies, *especially* the Catholic Church.

Séances were also an item of interest to me during my quest for spiritual enlightenment. These strange sessions of contacting those who had "gone beyond the veil" seemed odd and contrived to me. New Age peer pressure dictated that I maintained an open mind. The open mind was the vanguard of the counter culture. If your mind was closed you were not a member of the 'enlightened crowd.'

Spirit guides were quite popular among New Agers. If you advanced far enough to contact these beings of higher intelligence and enlightenment, then you also would be enlightened. There were many New Age authors/teachers who would expound about the Universal Masters and how they could help us earthlings. The Masters supposedly had accumulated knowledge known in the unseen world of power. The main conduit was a practice called automatic writing. This involved taking a pen and allowing the spirit being to write through your hand. Many of the books written about New Age ideas came to the authors through these means. Deception was routine in the New Age movement. There was no guiding light to tell you what was truth and what was false. Much was complete fabrication and some manipulation. When I actually crossed the line into the "real" dark beings, I did not know. Like most of my contemporaries, I didn't care about truth. We taught each other that truth was relative. I was blinded by my own desires during this time of my life. I was soon to learn that these beings were real but they were not who I was led to believe they were. When I did find out, it was almost too late. I needed to be rescued to avert a swirling force of destruction that wanted to literally kill me. I still remember the day my bedroom door opened by itself and *spirit beings* entered my body. I felt a physical prickling going up my arms and my legs. It was freaky.

An unusual event took place one sunny day when I was

walking barefoot down State Street in Madison, Wisconsin. This downtown area was famous during the counter culture. It contained all of the pot paraphernalia, occult books, incense, weird sex art, organic food bistros, and the Who's Who in the hippie world. I was with Claudia at the time. I was barefoot; this was normal footwear for flower children.

After jetting into McDonald's to grab a cup of java, we walked out onto the street when I stepped on something sharp, a piece of broken glass. My foot stung fiercely and was bleeding. Claudia applied first aid by first dousing hot coffee on the wound and then she placed her hand on this nasty cut pronouncing a prayer for a psychic healing to take place. I remember thinking, "Wow, I didn't know she was also a healer."

"This came from a curse," Claudia explained. "Just as you stepped on the glass, I saw two of my enemies with black power hurrying down the street. I think the curse was intended for me but it went to you." I knew Claudia had enemies, as she would refer to them occasionally. She insisted that her power was white power for good. Her enemies, however, conducted evil schemes *against* people. These were the Satanists.

This certainly was an exciting turn of events in a strange sort of way. During the hours' drive home from Madison, I was aware of pain in my foot every few miles. The next day at work, I was sitting at my desk, and had taken my shoes off to relax for a few minutes. As I crossed my wounded foot to rest on my other knee, I was startled to see the perfect shape of a sickle as the only remaining evidence of the larger cut from the broken glass. Even in my young naivety, I knew that a sickle was a satanic symbol. The initial wound was almost healed but the sickle remained. I shuddered inwardly. *"What have I gotten myself into anyway?"*

The entire event caused alarm, but did not deter my

obsession with the New Age rage. A couple of weeks later, my foot continued to be in considerable pain. I decided something was wrong and went to see a doctor who took an X-ray to find that a piece of glass remained inside my foot. He gave me a local anesthetic and then skillfully sliced my foot open to retrieve a shard of glass! I was not impressed with psychic healing.

CHAPTER 2

Problems Precipitated

What would cause a promising young woman to be driven to end it all!? Anyone who has experienced this tormenting pit knows it does not happen in an instant but is a slow brew of many factors and perceptions. It usually includes issues rooted deeply in the person's psyche which have helped shape their life and decisions. The main consistent factor, however, is always a loss of personal hope.

I, Patricia Ann Solveson, was and remain a classic baby boomer. I was born in 1951 and graduated from high school in 1969. *Sixty-nine is mighty fine* was our class motto. Some of my contemporaries may recall that 69 was the symbol of free sex in our brave new world of cultural revolution. I was a perfect fit for this crazy movement that began in the 60s as an antiwar campaign and led to a complete revolt of all known human institutions and morays by most people under 30. There was a collective mindset with the boomers that there existed a serious double standard in the society that we found ourselves a part of, as we emerged into young adulthood. Hypocrisy was another watchword thrown about religiously as we would sit in our circles smoking weed and drinking Coors beer. We agreed that something in our society was broken and needed fixing. We began to create our own reality: no restraints, no limits. Freedom to decide for ourselves what would shape our lives and our futures. We were courageous and outrageous. We relished in our reputation of being rebels against all forms of authority. As with most generations, we taught each other about life primarily through experimentation. This was a rich but dubious smorgasbord of deception and partial truth. Only time would test our maverick decisions on what life was really about.

When I graduated from High School, my ego had been sufficiently bruised by peer rejection and typical teen rivalries that left me bitter and feeling like an outsider. I desperately wanted to get on the bandwagon with a new identity: hippie, flower child, yeah, I liked it. I will never forget my last day of high school. As I literally bolted out of the school building, I spun around just as I reached the parking lot and threw my middle finger in that direction as a final farewell. So very angry and rebellious as a teenager, I had no idea at that time what lay smoldering beneath the surface of my soul.

To most, we seemed like a normal family. No one in the church community or even the extended family, with the exception of one aunt, knew about my mother's frequent states of deep depression. It is similar to the dysfunction caused by an alcoholic in the family. The lives of the family members revolve around the person with the addiction, their mood swings, and intimidating behavior. In our case, however, it was not alcohol but regular debilitating bouts of depression of a parent that imprinted all in our family. I was the most affected, although my sister Sue may contend with me on this assertion.

We lived in a nice, middle class, white house with redwood shutters. Our house was located on an acre and a half of rural land lined with elm trees and maples. When we moved out to the country, I was just three years old. Our family grew in size. In addition to my older brother Tommy, there were my two younger sisters, Susie and Mary, followed by Johnny. We had a big yard with trees and flowers that mom had planted and lots of room to run. I recall spending hours a day playing in our large square sandbox that my dad had constructed. I also remember playing 'make believe' mostly with Sue who is one and a half years younger than I. We would often play 'house' or 'Mickey and Minnie' as we pretended to be the Disney characters personified for hours on end.

As a child, I wouldn't have known what was normal and what wasn't. When we were all dressed up for Sunday Mass at our local parish, we seemed like everyone else. We were a good Catholic family. I was sent to parochial school for eight grades and was taught by nuns, as were my siblings. We went to Mass every day at St. Boniface School. My identity was a good little Catholic girl, even though I saw God as a rather mean God who was easy to displease.

We had mandatory confessions to the parish priest on a weekly basis. "I disobeyed my parents three times this week, Father. I am sorry for my sins." The priest would say something like: "Your penance is one 'Our Fathers' and three 'Hail Mary's.'" We were taught that repeating Catholic prayers was a way to repent for our sins. The Catholic sisters who taught in the school were educated, pious women. I respected most of them, while a few terrified me. Their reputation for strictness put fear in a young student's heart for good reason. I recall getting rapped on my knuckles for something which dimmed in contrast to the shock of this physical punishment. Any child in their right mind would avoid the Sisters' reprimands at all costs. One incident I can recall was during a daily Mass, as we were all waiting in total silence, when I accidentally bumped the kneeler in front of me with my foot. It released a loud reverberating bang. Oh no! I could already hear the scolding, think fast! I turned and looked at the child behind me in utter disgust and an audible "tsk." Sure enough, the Sister stormed up from the rear and confronted the student who was sitting behind me. I laugh as I recall this; apparently this good little Catholic girl could be devious when the situation required it. But as with most Catholics, my propensity to feel guilty was well developed and I felt terrible about it for years.

My father, a son of Lithuanian immigrants, was hard-working and devoted to his family of five children. His name was Joe. He was employed for many years at the Harley Davidson plant in Milwaukee. Although he had earned only an eighth-grade school diploma in the northern Wisconsin village where he grew up with his parents, his innate intelligence carried him to many promotions until he became a quality control engineer in the company. In fact, he was given a new Harley Davidson motorcycle every few years which transported him to and from work. He would ride his Harley through hail, sleet, and even snow every work day of the year. In the winter months he would add a side car for balance on the icy roads and wear a white snow suit. He was dubbed the abominable snowman by locals. Our dad Joe became an enigma in our town. My siblings and I would hear that roar of the engine coming from a mile away when it was time for him to come home from work. Most days we would go charging for the shed in the back of the house where he kept the motorcycle. We heard him coming and would run to welcome him with hugs and hellos.

My mother was a sensitive individual with a huge heart. Her life was her kids, and the Catholic Church that we were anchored into. When she was feeling well, she was a diligent housekeeper, cook, and baker. When family or friends would visit on a Sunday afternoon, she was the life of the party. She was compassionate and she reached out to people with her understanding and sympathy whenever she was able to.

My mother was intelligent and had wonderful talents. She had been involved in the theatre in the days of her youth. Though she had not attended college, she worked in various offices as a proofreader and transcriptionist, a demanding job requiring her to track with fast-paced executives. Intelligent, and always knowledgeable about current affairs, mom could discuss notable politicians and ideologies of the day. Her father died when she was only five years old. Not having a father was her most painful reality as she grew up. Often I pondered my mother's upbringing and her family history to see if there was any glaring reason for my mother's chronic states of depression.

CHAPTER 3

Recipe for Trouble

Valerie Ann, a delicate flower, was born in the United States, and was the eighth surviving child of Slovenian immigrants. Five of her siblings died in infancy or early childhood. I could not imagine what it must have been like to lose five children to death. Peter and Maria had been peasant farmers in the foothills of the majestic Slovenian Alps. Life was extremely difficult for them. My grandfather would often take off from the farm to find other means of income. He made several trips to the US and would be absent for long periods. This did not sit well with the matriarch of the family. Weary of running a failing farm on a rocky untillable plot of soil, she put out an ultimatum to her husband. *"If you leave again you must take us with you or don't bother coming back at all!"* Although we do not know all the details, the farm was put up for sale and passage, the lowest fare, to America was booked on the new, grandiose, unsinkable luxury ocean liner, *the Titanic.* My grandfather knew that his property was not prime real estate and would likely take a long time to sell, even years. Because of this, he purchased passage for America on the Titanic well over a year in advance. But when the farm sold sooner than anyone expected, the big family packed and was ready to roll before the Titanic was completely finished.

They exchanged their tickets for the Titanic to that of the Olympia, which was another of the luxury ocean liners of the White Star Line that was set to launch on her maiden voyage on May 31, 1911. They would sail out on the high seas for 14 days to meet a new and vastly contrasting world to their poor Slovenian homestead. Captain Edward Smith was the skipper of this incredible sea vessel. He sailed the Olympia with my grandparents and their children safely to New York Harbor on May 14, 1911. Captain Smith later commanded the maiden voyage of the Titanic and was lost at sea with the majority of the 1,320 passengers and 907 crew. Seven hundred and five survived the disaster in life boats. To this day when I hear about the Titanic or read about that fateful night, my stomach churns and my pulse rate speeds up. With the awareness of this stark twist of events in the lives of my ancestors, it surely gives me pause to stop and contemplate the grand plan for my life and ultimate destiny.

Maria, my maternal grandmother, was a strong religious woman who sang all the time, according to my mother. My parents lived with my grandmother when the first three of five children were born. We lived upstairs in a few rooms. When you are only three, you don't understand a lot of what happens around you, but I remember it was a crisis in our entire family when she died. Vague memories of what was most likely grief and loss are still in my conscious memory. Maria's strong matriarchal ways resulted in a big change when she no longer ruled over the house. My mother loved her dearly, yet there were some mysteries about their relationship too. My mother told me that there was a time in her childhood that her mother tried to keep her hidden. I still am puzzled by this. My mother had many fears and anxieties in her life. Was this the reason? I could not understand why this would have been. But neither did I understand why my mother had a nervous breakdown when she was only 18 years old. Coupled with some other odd behaviors when my mother was elderly, it seemed quite obvious to me and my sisters that there is much we were never told. In my opinion, my mother's depressions were undoubtedly rooted in the family skeletons that remain in the closet to this day.

The same skeletons came to life in my own closet when later in life, memories emerged that forced me to examine events in my early childhood relative to my grandmother in which trauma became trapped in my pre-verbal emotions. I always seemed to know that something had happened to me in that big old house where I lived until I was three. I can recall saying to my siblings that something 'bad' happened in that house. But I was not able to state what that bad thing was. At least I didn't know in my conscious mind. The day would come however, when I would confront the issue and validate the traumatic event for the sake of my own healing.

When the bedroom door was closed, it was a warning that my mother was in a depression. I would usually go in quietly. "Mommy?" Her voice would be higher than normal and she would tell me to go and play; at other times she would perceive my worry about her and try to reassure me that she would be okay soon. I am quite certain that she had panic attacks along with her depressed state. She would be in a state of hyper fear. Her breathing would become rapid and her hands would begin to go numb. If our dad was not available, she would call for me in a frantic voice and tell me to massage her hands. She would be half crying and half hyperventilating. I would rub her hands and worry about her state of mind, never knowing what was causing this suffering. Her depressions could last for hours or days. I am quite sure she also suffered from migraine headaches along with the depression.

After baby brother was born, the bouts of depression kept my mom from being able to care for Johnny at times.

She relied on me to feed and change diapers when she could not function. I enjoyed this role at times. There was one day when sitting in my classroom, someone came to pick me up, although I cannot recall who that someone was. But I was escorted home to take care of Johnny because she was unable to get out of bed due to a severe state of depression. I was happy to leave school that day. It made me feel important. Later I realized the circumstances of my childhood had forced me to grow up before my time. Taking on too much responsibility became a way of life for me later. In fact, I seemed to bear the weight of depression myself at times. I believe this stunted my emotional and social growth as well. It was a load I was not equipped to carry. It resulted in poor self-esteem and much fear about the future. I did not tell anyone for many years that during my school years, I had a fear that one day I would get off the school bus to find that my mother had hanged herself. The dark cloud left unspoken affected me. I lived with my fears and the sorrow of seeing my mother hurt like that. My broken heart sunk deep down inside as I tried to cope with life. When I needed my mother to teach me about life, and to tell my troubles to, I felt very alone. My independence grew stronger to meet the need created by the lack of guidance.

Most of our active play took place with our dad. He would have us outside playing ball or pulling weeds. During the winter months, one of my fondest memories was skating on the Menomonie River not far from our house. Learning the basics of ice skating soon lent to playing a rough game of hockey with a lot of falling down and laughing.

When my mother was not depressed, we had good times all together. We would go on camping trips and visit with relatives. We celebrated all the holidays in grand fashion. On Easter we took part in the solemn Catholic services which, on Easter Sunday morning, gave way to the happiness of finding our colorful Easter baskets laden with chocolate marshmallow eggs and jelly beans on a bed of green cellophane grass. Baking the ethnic Slovenian bread of Poticia, buttery dough with rich creamy walnut filling, was a ritual both parents performed and the kids helped out too. I looked forward to each of these holidays. Mom also took great measures to celebrate each of our birthdays. To this day we celebrate family birthdays in the same style. I think the holidays and birthdays helped her with her own suffering. She would seem to try more, not wanting to disappoint us on those special days of the year; truly, they were a reprieve from the underlying sadness that marked my childhood. Why does it seem that the people with the deepest capacity to love and live are often the most assailed by this cruel world? I loved my mother deeply but the mounting bitterness kept me from expressing it until later in my life.

Big problems erupted when I began to mature physically. My development, along with the natural hormonal peaks and valleys, set the stage for tumultuous years of a combative mother-daughter relationship. My mother could not cope with my assertive behavior nor my experimentation with 'all things feminine.' Wearing blue jeans to church became a regular battlefield. Wearing eye makeup started a literal war of the wills. Mom became more overprotective and controlling than any time previously. In the absence of being taught about womanhood, I took the bull by the horns and plunged in on my own. Every step of independence was met with vehement resistance. Her way of dealing with me was through emotional outbursts. The extreme emotional reactions were designed to keep me in line with her conservative ideas about how her blossoming daughter should grow up. She had an image of a good Catholic girl in her mind—an image that I shattered repeatedly.

When these battles for independence would take place,

my mother would literally scream at me for long periods. She would say, *"How can you do this to me? Why can't you just do as I say?" "People will think we are terrible parents letting you dress this way!"* I would have strong feelings of guilt that I was causing all of my mother's problems. It did not help that my dad began to blame me for inflaming her condition as well. It just reinforced the lie that I was responsible. Her raging, combined with the guilt, began to produce an uncontrollable rebellion inside. By the time I was sixteen I had built tall and strong walls around my heart. I was starved for emotional intimacy. Somewhere deep inside, the voice of a little girl that had been crying for her mommy was silenced forever.

CHAPTER 4

Dubious Diversions

Around the time of my 15th birthday, an interesting turn of events took place. One-quarter mile down the road from our house, a new family moved in and they had horses. I loved horses. I had a pony that was the joy of my life. My parents tried hard to demonstrate their love and give me what I wanted in life. I had begged for a horse. The pony was pretty close to fulfilling this particular dream. He was a large Welsh pony that could be ridden. His name was Buddy. I spent much time with him and riding him. He was well behaved most of the time. However, each time I would urge him into a gallop, he would begin to kick up his heels and I would often go flying to the ground. My temper would flare at these times and I would try to give him a swat. He was always ready for me and would take off running before I had a firm hold of the reins. *"Nooooo!"* I would yell and go running after him until he slowed or stopped to munch. I was grateful to have Buddy nevertheless. His companionship kept me from the utter loneliness I felt inside.

When the neighbors moved in one-quarter mile down the highway, I saw their beautiful Quarter horses romping in the corral. My imagination ran wild: real horses, not ponies. How I wished I could be close to those beautiful beasts. I began to make a plan to become acquainted with the neighbors. After all, I had considerable babysitting experience. Perhaps they were in need of my services and just maybe I could have a window to the world of registered Quarter horses.

My entire world was turned upside down when I began to babysit for the new neighbors. This family shattered my world of religious overprotection. The kids were monsters, the parents smoked, swore, and drank all kinds of liquor. Once the shock wore off and my sensibilities were permanently dismantled, I started to love this family. Their unruly, raw lives were fascinating to me in a way. When I was with them, I felt like I could be more myself, although I had no idea who I was. I began to explore life a little. I began to think there was something else 'out there' besides rules, sorrow, and guilt. I also began to smoke cigarettes and drink beer. I escaped to their house as often as I could manage.

I became the regular babysitter and poured a lot of love into those precious rascals. I was even given the opportunity to help with the horses. These were show horses. I helped groom them, ride them, and later went to weekend horse shows. It was an exciting diversion from my home life. The mom of this family was to become my best friend a few years later. But as therapeutic as this relationship was at first, later the loose lifestyle took root and I accepted some bad habits and attitudes that played a role in my downward spiral.

In addition to the happy diversion down the road, another bright spot in my youth was my propensity toward creativity and art. My gift of creativity was apparent to all around me. When I was eight years old, I had received a Jon Nagy Art Kit for Christmas. The kit contained sketching paper and various shades of gray pastels, along with instructions. As I began to delve into drawing, I discovered success. Accurate likenesses of dogs, horses and other animals emerged in my sketch book. The family was impressed and very encouraging to me. With each new sketch I received praise from my parents. This strong reinforcement certainly played a role in bringing forth a God-given talent.

I took art classes each of my four years of high school. I even placed in the high school art show. On special occasions such as birthdays and anniversaries, I would find something to paint on, canvas, rocks, or a nice piece of wood, and give my artwork as gifts. Thankfully the recipients always seem to sincerely enjoy my tokens of love. To this day when I walk in my relatives' homes, I see my artwork gracing their walls.

CHAPTER 5

Stumbling Through the Teen Years

High school was a battleground. A battle in which I felt I had been defeated. I was not a member of the 'in crowd,' though I thought I should be. The popular kids would associate with me but they would not include me as an insider. Because of family rules I was not allowed to date until I was 16 years old. When the junior varsity basketball star asked me to dance at the Friday night hop, I melted under the power of his rapt attention. After a few dances on the gymnasium floor and a few passionate kisses, Ron was madly in love with me.

This torrid first romance took my world from shades of bland to a kaleidoscope of emotions that I did not know I possessed. The first night we necked in the gym. (Here is a term one does not hear often today!) Necking, yes, passionate and repeated kissing on the lips and elsewhere. But there we were, unashamed. We continued our romance in the halls of the school and after games and at dances. That is until the inevitable came. He wanted to date. This meant driving his souped up glossy Camaro to pick me up and take me places. Most likely those destinations would end up in the back seat of that shiny car. My parents feared this and so put an abrupt halt to my first romance. "No, you may not date until you are sixteen."

My boyfriend was apparently a little bit more in love with himself than me. He wanted to show off a girl and his wonderful set of wheels so he politely dumped me and found a different girlfriend. She happened to be one of the cutest cheerleaders on the squad in addition to being a brain. Oh, did I mention she was very popular with *everyone*? I had the painful experience of watching them flirt and make out in the halls for quite some time.

The unresolved hurt and anger began to grow rather than heal. Phonographs were now becoming available to all economic classes at a reasonable price. I remember my beautiful new 45 record player. It became my closest friend. *I'll Do My Crying in the Rain* by the Everly Brothers went round and round on that turntable. Leslie Gore's hit song: *It's My Party and I'll Cry If I Want To*, and on it went with my very real lament. I had forsaken some of my best friends in pursuit of a boyfriend. What a mistake that was. Now I was swimming upstream alone, dejected and rejected, hating my world more than ever.

It was about that time that a new girl moved to town. She was stocky and plain in appearance. But I recall the first day I greeted her. We were in the locker room after everybody's favorite—gym class. She returned my greeting and I saw a spark that had not been there a few moments earlier. Joyce and I became friends in that instant. We came from a similar family background. We liked the same things, and we each had a wild side. We liked to sneak cigarettes and eventually alcohol. We would spend hours discussing everything imaginable in our world of emerging adulthood. She saved the day for me during those discouraging times of my sophomore and junior years of high school. My rebellion did not disappear, however; it just went into hiding for a while, attempting and succeeding in redoubling its strength.

Joyce and I both hung out a lot at the ranch up the road.

We would share the babysitting jobs and we would hit the liquor cupboard on a regular basis. I remember the very first night I ever drank alcohol. We planned to spend the night since the parents of our charges would not get home until the wee hours. We got the darlings to sleep and raided the cupboard. There were many choices. We decided that the cherry-flavored brandy smelled pretty good. We filled out kitchen tumblers up and began to drink to the last drop. In about 30 minutes, I was dizzy and hanging on the toilet bowl. So, this is what it was like to drink, I thought. Why my mother picked that particular night to call and check on me I will never know. She really did not check so often anymore, even though she always discouraged me from going to the neighbors. She knew something was up as soon I spoke my first slurred word: "Hullo-o." She sent my dad down to pick me up immediately. I heard a long lecture featuring various volumes of yelling and crying by my mother and a few sharp reprimands from Dad as well. I was forced to go to the confessional booth at our church in the morning so I could repent from my sin. It was just a symptom, however, of a deeper need that no one realized I had, even me. I stopped drinking brandy at least for a while. Beer was just as fine, better in fact.

When I graduated from high school, I was ill-equipped for handling life. I had no idea what I wanted out of life. I knew I had art abilities. I did not feel I had the confidence to go to college. Neither were the girls in the family encouraged or financed to go to college, only my brothers were. I attempted to pursue developing my art ability; however, too much of my energy was taken with fighting off depression and mind battles. I was striving to fit into a world that I did not really know how to live in. I did not even make it through the first semester.

After various jobs, I decided to try school again, this

time for child development. I loved children and thought I could work in daycare or preschool settings. After a year of school I got a certificate which led me to a job with emotionally disturbed children. I received additional training and moved up in the ranks. I found something I was successful at. I poured myself into this job.

I was maturing, now 22 years old, but that did not mean I was making all good choices. I drank and smoked pot with my latest friends. The counterculture was in full swing now. I had moved out of my childhood home, first living with a boyfriend and when we broke up, my co-worker and I shared an apartment. Living on my own was exciting. After 20 years of wearing the cumbersome yoke of my mother's problems, I felt free! Stuffing all of the old concern and feelings of guilt, I purchased an expensive powder blue 10-speed bike with sleek lines and a built-in tire pump. I accessorized with a generator light so I could bike day and night if I wanted. 'Blue Boy' is what I dubbed my new toy. Riding this gem, hair blowing back, and free, gave me a feeling of happiness. There was no boyfriend in the picture at that time. I didn't need one. I just wanted freedom.

CHAPTER 6

Love at First Sight

I was outside on a sunny and windy March afternoon with the kids in my unit, which were the youngest at the Residential Center for emotionally disturbed children where I was employed. I looked across the big lawn and saw another youth counselor with the junior boys unit. They were playing some type of ball game. The staffer caught my attention because I had not recalled seeing him before. There were approximately 40 employees working at the center. My co-unit counselor was with me at the time of this first sighting. I said to her, "Who is that? I have never seen him before!" Her answer was lost in the haze as I saw this handsome young man decked out in faded blues: a jean jacket and pants, and a big frock of platinum blonde hair falling down on the side of his face. Although I could not make out his facial features, it was his demeanor and stance that swept me away. There was a seriousness, yet an innocence that surrounded him. I made up my mind to meet him somewhere, somehow, and soon.

Carl Edward Solveson was hired along with a lot of other baby boomers at this facility. We comprised the treatment staff for these children with autism, childhood schizophrenia, and other behavioral disorders who needed residential care. The sizable staff, which numbered over 50, were either paraprofessionals with some education or held one college degree or another. There was an in-house comprehensive training program for all employees that I sank my intellectual teeth into. Once trained by the multidisciplinary treatment team of mental health professionals, we would implement the individual plans for the children in the living unit.

The work was not boring and the salaries were respectable. In addition to implementing the daily programs, we occasionally had to wrestle down bigger kids who lost complete control of their behavior and became combative. One day when I was substituting on the senior girls unit for another youth counselor, I heard some commotion and hurried down the hall. As I did, I was ambushed from two directions, one angry girl in front of me and one who leaped on my back from behind. I began to yell for help, which came quickly.

On another occasion, I entered a room where a staffer, a tiny little thing, was being held hostage by a big 13-year-old wielding two table forks. His eyes were bugging out of his head as he threatened to use the forks for harm. I froze when I entered the room. I tried not to panic and attempted to recall my training techniques. As we stood in total silence, motionless, the other counselor began to softly sing, "Raindrops Keep Falling On My Head." As she sang, the boy's arms came down in slow motion. A third counselor, a man, entered and then used a little muscle to disarm the situation. Working at the center provided a certain adrenaline level which often came in handy. This work was interesting and fulfilling. I was extremely ambitious in my workplace. I continued to be educated through extensive training with therapists. I conducted play therapy under the supervision of a psychiatric team and rose to the position of unit supervisor of the youngest children in the facility. All of the staff under my supervision had college degrees, two had master degrees. What I lacked in formal education I compensated for by my diligence and ability to apply the treatment modalities. I had natural leadership abilities and I was motivated to prove myself at all times. I excelled at my job until the politics of the treatment center put me in a position of opposition to the administration. I reacted vehemently when I witnessed corruption at the top levels of management. My altruistic idealism caused me to resign rather than compromise.

The social life spawned by workplace associates was priceless. I spent many hours with friends sharing beers and shop talk. The high class downtown bar became our second home. One could enter on any given afternoon or evening and find two to ten coworkers, kicking back with a brew, waiting for the next hot issue to develop at work. It was a good time. I had found acceptance as well as a handsome lover.

Like all good hippies, Carl and I fell in love and fell into bed at the same time. Throwing morality to the wind, we freely engaged in sex without even a hint of guilt. We lived together for approximately one year and then got married. In the early seventies, cohabitation was not accepted by most in society as it is today. It was quite taboo then and we were pioneers along with most of the rest of our generation.

Neither set of parents knew that we were living together. We did not see our families very much in those days. We were all on a quest to disassociate with the establishment and our families were part of that abhorred institution. But that did not mean that they had no influence in our lives. Carl received a call one day from his mother confronting him about a rumor she had heard that he was living in fornication. When he hung up and told me, I could hear the mild panic in his voice. We sat together at our kitchen table and as best as I can recall we said it at about the same time, *"We may as well GET MARRIED."* We could come up with no reason why we shouldn't marry.

When Carl's mother called to confirm or deny the rumor that her son was living with a girl, our drive to tie the knot was accelerated by the fear that *my* parents would find out. This was even more troublesome because of my mother's fragile emotional state. I did not want to cause a breakdown, nor did I want to face my dad if my actions caused my mother to become more depressed. Since the time I moved out of my home at age 21, I had very little contact with my parents or my siblings. Prior to our marriage, Carl and I both were guilty of living a double life. Our parents had no idea about the dangerous conduct that had emerged in our lives.

Carl had been a Marine and served in the Vietnam War. It was there that the drug habit took hold of him. Drugs and alcohol were the ways many of the troops attempted to keep their sanity in the insane conditions they experienced in Vietnam. Carl came back from his time overseas with an attitude of tough indifference that revealed itself in conduct regardless of life. Shortly before I met Carl, he had wrapped his car around a telephone pole at a moment when he was so high on drugs that he literally did not feel any pain. It was a miracle that he survived this accident without serious injury.

Carl served in the Marine Corps for four years. He had been honorably discharged with the rank of sergeant. But he was a heavy drinker throughout his service and had used drugs habitually to survive the insanity of his year in Vietnam. So, coming home, he continued this regimen in an attempt to numb the trauma of all he had done and seen there. Carl was tough, strong and silent. His natural bent was on the introverted side, but the effects of the war made him retreat all the more. His father had not only been a quiet man, but more truthfully, a silent man. He gave little or no input into the lives of his four children as he worked the farm which he eventually lost. The family moved to town, but his father never fully recovered from this loss. Carl was only too happy to escape the stricken atmosphere of his home by enlisting in the Marines.

We planned our wedding in three weeks with a very small budget. I had a simple long white dress made by a friend that was set off by a large brim white picture hat. My adorable hat was graced with a crown of fresh daisies. Carl wore a powder blue tux with black trim. He looked dashing with his long blond hair and shy smile. I remember feeling very irritable on my wedding day. It was the hottest day of the year with humidity off the charts. I felt a lot of mental pressure being with my family who scarcely knew the real me anymore.

After the church segment we all drove to a nice supper club for a meal. My guests were mainly family and a few close friends. We did not include most of our counter culture friends as that would have been way too unpredictable with our families around us. After the meal and a few gifts, the torrid day turned rapidly into a fierce thunderstorm including high winds and hail. All the guests headed home, except for the bride and groom. We wanted to celebrate in our own fashion and stopped at a bar/bowling alley only about a mile from our apartment. We drank our beers and relaxed together and laughed. We had a little surprise though. After our second round, a small boisterous group of older folks came into the establishment. As I glanced their way, I saw a couple that I recognized. "Carl, look who just came in!" I tried to disappear into the bar top but our wedding apparel made us stand out. Abruptly our landlords approached us to greet us. "We thought you were already married!" they exclaimed. Our clothes gave us away. "Nope," we shyly replied. We were found out. We had lied and said we were married so that they would rent the apartment to us. It was embarrassing but we laughed about it a few years later.

We continued to work at the treatment center for kids, but we had a dream. We wanted to move out of the city and go to a less densely populated area to live. We both loved the outdoors and desired to do what many flower children dreamed about—live off the land! This was a whole different level of our beloved counter culture which meant retreating from the established way of life handed down to us. 'Living off the land' was a popular expression with the baby booming crowd. Getting away from all of societal norms and expectations was a goal. Getting in touch with nature and our natural desires as opposed to the nine-to-five culture sounded like a realistic goal to us. What was stopping us? We had no real responsibilities. We were resourceful and we had young love to propel us. We felt invincible!

CHAPTER 7

Pioneers of the Northwoods

We had only been married for one year when we loaded up Carl's silvery blue chariot, a Chevy Impala complete with a glass pack, (a modified muffler that made a nice roar when he hit the gas). We hitched up my parent's pop-up camper behind the car, and drove more than three hundred miles to the north. We had purchased a 20-acre parcel on a tiny lake in the woods way up in the northwestern corner of the Wisconsin wilderness. Our first building project was an outhouse, which we built with an open front and a view of our little lake through the oaks and poplar trees. No need for a door since there were no people or houses for quite a distance. We were 'nature children.' We carried our water from town in a big old milk can and bathed in the neighboring lake, which substituted for a bathtub. Together we worked on all the aspects of building a simple walkout basement.

There were regular visits with a couple of our other hippie friends who had also moved up to the area. We would exchange labor as we built our handmade houses and have a party every time we did. We sat around a fireplace, or campfire, smoked weed, drank beer while discussing details of the latest building challenge as we listened to Frank Zappa, the Doobie and the Allman Brothers, with a little Melanie,

Baez and Carly Simon thrown into the mix. Smoking pot together, in addition to drinking a considerable amount of bourbon, beer, and Boone's Farm was commonplace. So what could possibly be wrong with this picture? We were living the dream of the baby boomer generation, starting a new life and getting high whenever possible.

My excitement to be on our own land kept me happy for quite a while. Our 20-acre parcel was a long strip of wooded terrain. Our small fishing lake was visible through the dense coniferous forest. It was a beautiful view and I would sit and just look at it for long periods. We had frontage on this lake and we were so proud of that, even though the lake was only 14 acres in size. We had many varieties of pine trees and a few hardwood trees. There were many poplar trees and some birch as well. The wind gusting through those leaves creates a sound of soft clapping that was music to my ears. To us, it was paradise and we could feel the freedom under our feet. It was a whole new world for us, vastly different from the city life we experienced in southern Wisconsin. We relished in the isolation of our land. We were located on a gravel road which was one half mile off of the nearest paved road. Our driveway was one half mile long as it wound gently into the dense trees.

Our dwelling was to be built in two steps. We would begin by building a cement block walk-out basement, and then as we could afford it, the wooden A-frame would be built on top. Living in the camper was a delight, at least at first. On most nights we would have a campfire and then retire to our little bed space as we listened to whippoorwills and howling coyotes. I was not afraid with my prince charming at my side. On the rainy nights, I can still hear the rat-a-tat of the windblown raindrops falling hard on the metal roof of the camper—more music. We did not have a care in the world. But after a couple of months of this kind of life, the day came when the lack of space was driving me crazy. After making a delicious tuna and noodle salad for the workers and serving them, I turned to finally sit and eat and sat squarely on top of my own plate of tuna salad. With a hoot, I jumped up amid the laughter of my friends. That was the last straw. When the day came to move into the capped basement, I was so relieved, nothing else mattered to me. I had a home.

We barely beat the winter north winds as the lake froze and the snow flurries began to swirl. We outfitted our little basement home with a few pieces of furniture, drapes on the windows of the exposed side and a pot belly wood stove.

Deer hunting rifle season is serious in the north woods of Wisconsin. The woods are overflowing with wildlife, particularly whitetail deer. Just before opening day of our very first deer season, we had a heavy snow. Just as the snow began to fall, we drove to town to purchase some needed supplies. By the time we returned we could barely make it down our dirt road and then down our one half mile long driveway. The snow was piling up quickly and it was blowing hard. We were very happy to make it home without getting hopelessly stuck in a snow drift in the middle of the road. We had filled our car with all kinds of supplies so we did not mind being snowed in one bit. It was all part of the big adventure. The snow continued to pile up over the next two days. After the snow stopped and the morning sun shone brightly, Carl made a trip out to our homespun outhouse. Carl relaxed as he routinely did, but suddenly heard a gun being cocked. He was surprised to discover a hunter decked in blaze orange standing within earshot of the outhouse. The next day we had someone banging on our door. It was another hunter who thought we might need help because of the deep snow.

The winter was a challenge but we survived it. We ran out of our savings and had to look for jobs. We found work at a county program for adults and children with various handicaps. This employment put us back into society to some degree but we had to eat. We were not ignorant that "living off the land" was a bit unrealistic but we found that just moving away from the city was already a large part of our dream. We did not really mind the work.

Though our lives had become fairly predictable, I had begun to feel depressed. The excitement of moving to a new location, and all the activity of the building, was beginning to wear off. We had left life-long friends and of course all family to come to a new life. It was not just a transitory melancholia, it had a sense of uneasiness with it. It felt like old ghosts had come back to haunt me and I was not sure why. This turned out to be more literal than I could have imagined at the time.

CHAPTER 8

A Looming Dark Cloud

As the sun set over the north woods, the glow of it came through the trees. I stood motionless. The silhouette of Jack and Red pine trees appeared black against the sky. This fading amber light was beautiful. The growing dusk of the evening sent a shiver of dread and gloom over my soul. Why did it feel like a dark cloud had enveloped my life for no apparent reason? The feeling was like a strange mixture of despair mixed with fearfulness. As I thrust it out, I was aware that with each passing night I felt less able to resist this. Could this feeling overtake me? I shuddered to think of it.

What is happening to me?! Depression pulled at my emotions and I was becoming increasingly concerned. I was happy, wasn't I? I had everything to live for. We lived in the beautiful north country now. My marriage was good. We still drank and smoked too much but didn't everyone? I had a good job. In fact I worked in the mental health field with children and adults who had special needs. I knew plenty of professional counselors and therapists, personally. But I did not want to ask for their help. I was way too proud for that. I always tried to make the appearance that I had it "all together."

Although I had not sought out any local psychics, I had

heard of someone with psychic powers who owned a bar not too far away. Perhaps I needed to go and look this person up. I mulled this over but for some strange reason I did not feel the old attraction to this world any longer. I had a real life now and did not necessarily want to continue in this pseudo life form.

As the depression grew more ominous, I became very concerned. It seemed as though all of my fears were constantly in my face. My deepest emotional pain also came up to haunt me. It seemed like all of the pain of my 26 years came up full force and I couldn't run or hide from it. I began to have panic attacks! I did not have a name for this at that time. But a fear came that was so strong, it engulfed me and threatened to overwhelm my senses ... and my sanity. I felt as though I was about to lose control of my mind! This was terrifying to me.

There was one person who I remained in contact with through letters after our move. It was Cathy, the mother of the children I babysat for at the ranch down the road, so long ago. She was the horse mom who became a close friend in my late teens and early twenties. After I was married, she had become a person of faith—a Christian who loved Jesus. She would send me leaflets about the Bible and letters about giving my life to Jesus. Although I loved her dearly, this mail was extremely annoying to me. I finally wrote her and told her to *'Stop sending me that crap!'* But now my entire life was spinning wildly out of control. My days were spent in anxiety fearing the worst. I was floundering in a sea of fears and inner pain. I felt like I was drowning. I had nowhere to turn for help. I had no one to talk to. Carl cared but had no answers. The inner voice kept saying suicide was the way out. My life was becoming more painful than I could bear. I couldn't go on this way much longer. The panic attacks continued. That horrific spiraling feeling of despair claimed my emotional state. A mental picture of me dangling from a rope attached to our exposed rafters began to plague my days and nights.

Carl did not really know the depth of my torment. He continued to numb himself with a feisty marijuana habit. He was not aware that my condition was becoming dangerous.

Simultaneous to this mental torment I was experiencing, a very different realization took place. I became troubled about my moral condition. Although I feigned a caring personality, I realized that everything I did had a selfish motive. I hated myself for that. I really lived for myself and it was starting to make me feel like an egotistical and calloused person. I did nothing out of a motivation that showed I cared about others. If I showed consideration for others there was always something in it for me. The truth was, when not numbed with drugs or alcohol, I was bitter and did not like people a lot. *It was all an act!*

Nature was my 'thing' in those days. I loved to walk under the towering pines and glimpse the billowing cumulus clouds against the brilliant northern sky. The great outdoors was my comfort and my love. I had put people far away from my mind. My little world was fairly secure but outside of it, life seemed too terrifying for me to venture into. It was agonizing to think much about the past. There had been too much unresolved pain from my upbringing which left me confused and ill-prepared for life. I nursed a sense of personal rejection from various people along the way. I am sure some of it was because of my own rebellious and calloused attitude that had developed. Some of it was real emotional damage, plus a deep sorrow from growing up surrounded by depression and a constant demand for performance. When I was romping in through the trees and beholding a beautiful scene, my inner bitterness would illicit a curse if I saw a light from a house.

CHAPTER 9

Only One Knew

Walking down our long and densely wooded driveway, alone and afraid, the tears flowed. I didn't know what to do. The powerlessness brought on a prickly sensation running down my arms and legs, and rapid breathing belied the panic building inside. Perhaps a gun would have been more practical but I didn't really know how to shoot. All I could think of was ending the torment. I heard the clattering of the Popple leaves as the wind blew hard and whipped my tears into the air.

Cathy's letter came to my mind. *"Surrender to Jesus, give Him your life."* For weeks already I had been pushing her words out of my mind. I did not want religion. Didn't my family life and my mother's depression prove it was a false hope? I did not want to be a religious fanatic like Cathy.

Today was different. I had reached a level of sheer desperation. *"Surrender to Jesus, give Him your life"* echoed again. I began to reason, what did I really have to lose? My life is all screwed up any way. I don't want this life. Cathy's words did not go away. I pondered the meaning of surrendering to Jesus. Was he was even real? Maybe he was just a myth. Hopeless feelings washed over me and I felt nauseated. Out of sheer desperation, I prayed for the first time in many years. I sobbed and sputtered my prayer. *"Jesus, I don't even know if You are real, but if You are, then please help me before it is too late. I give You this messed up life. Here, take it!"* At that moment all of my objections to God or the existence of God or the gospel really did not matter. My pride was gone. All of my plans to do something important in my life had evaporated in a grey cloud of hopelessness. So what did it matter? I had no thoughts of being a sinner or that I should confess my wrongs, I winced and cried out for help from the God I did not know.

As I stood alone in my woodland cathedral, something began to happen. Only five minutes had passed since I had offered my simple prayer. Now my entire being was enveloped with light. I felt a growing presence of something good, like pure love. Like a dying person crawling in the hot desert sand, my spirit began to drink. All the sensations of panic and desperation faded as a strong feeling of love poured in. More than emotion, it was more like a substance that filled my entire being. The presence of God was unmistakable: surreal, not earthly. While I did not hear words in my head, I perceived a voice deep inside that said, *"Do not fear, I love you."* This powerful feeling of love permeated every cell of my being. In a moment in time I knew that God existed and that He cared about *me!*

Although it lasted only about ten minutes, the presence of God was unmistakable and I was touched in an irreversible way. How did I know this experience was God? It was all light and love, no mixture of the darkness I had known in the past. I walked back to the house as if in a dream.

This experience with Jesus took me into a new reality

that transcended time and space. I accepted this encounter and the hope that accompanied it though I did not understand it. The love I experienced in those moments carried me. It was as though something deep within me woke up! I became keenly aware of God and thought about Him a lot. The feelings of depression and destruction still came but now they would come in momentary waves. Each time I would call to Jesus inside and they would vanish for a time.

What happened to me and who is this God, who now seemed amazing in my eyes? I had to learn more about Him. Pulling the old dusty Bible out of a storage box in the corner of our basement dwelling, I read in random places. The Bible was a book that Catholics were not encouraged to read in my generation. I had gotten the impression that it was for scholars only. At that point I couldn't afford to care about what was said about the Bible. God had come to me in my darkest hour and I needed to know more about Him. He is the only one who could help me.

What I discovered in the Bible was positively amazing to me. The Psalms were an absolute treasure. I would read David's cries to God for help in all kinds of trouble. I found myself in David's woes. I drew much comfort from these words. The New Testament was a little uncomfortable because it made me feel hopeless in my obvious sinful condition. Although I had heard about the cross all my life, I had never really gotten the message of it. I was blinded that Jesus endured the cross for me and that I was forgiven because of love. I spent an entire childhood thinking I put him on that cross. I felt guilty about that. I felt guilty for my mother's depressions as well. Rebellion had been my own solution to all the guilt and sadness.

A few week later, I decided to write to Cathy and let her know her prayers had been answered. I wrote that I had asked the Lord to take over my life. I said I was wondering when

He would do this since now I had surrendered. She replied promptly and just a few days later when I ripped open her letter, the words she wrote set my spirit soaring. She said if I meant what I had said, then this loving Savior had already taken my life over to His control and that I must now believe by faith! No sooner had I read those words than a wave of something divine hit me. I literally felt a force of that same love I had felt in the woods combined with joy roll into me and lift me. I did not know until later that this is the moment I had been "born again." I was euphoric! I felt different. It had never occurred to me that God was someone who could be so personal with me. I had no idea that He loved me and could change me and change my life. Why did I run from Him for so long?

As I read more and more of the Bible I began to trust Him, at least a little. I still had a lot of fear and although the deep depression and suicidal thoughts abated, tormenting fears would dog my days off and on. During those uncomfortable times, I learned to pray. My prayer consisted of mostly three little words: *Jesus, help me!* And every time I would utter those three words, whether aloud or in my thoughts, I would have a bit of relief.

For two years, it was me and Jesus. I still recall the lyrics of a song by Andre Crouch. I sang it at least one hundred times: *Jesus is the answer for the world today, above Him there's no other, Jesus is the way*. It was like a honeymoon, a true vacation from all of the horrific war of life that had beset me so cruelly. I wanted it to last forever, but I realized (much later on) this special time was given as a gift—a time for faith to rise and trust to be rebuilt.

Carl was not sure what to make of the new me. I wanted him to have what I had received, but soon it was clear that no amount of prodding on my part could bring about real faith in Carl. I had to wait, hope, and trust that soon Carl would see it all for himself and want Jesus too.

About one year after I became a believer, Carl and our friend Phil were working on the structure of the A-frame upstairs one day. I was downstairs busying myself with the mundane when I heard and felt a loud crashing sound. *"What could that have been?"* A few minutes later, the door opened slowly and Phil appeared with Carl leaning on his shoulder. "He fell from the rafters but I think he is okay." Carl was moaning slightly and sat down on the sofa to recover. A cup of coffee and a short rest revived him nicely so he went back upstairs to resume working. Shortly, the door opened again, this time only Carl was there. *"Honey!* You have got to come upstairs and see this." He ran back and I scooted out the door behind him. As we entered the large main area of the A-frame construction, Carl pointed to two boards lying in the midst of chain saws, buck saws, drills, nails, and other assorted sharp and dangerous tools. "I fell on these two boards in the shape of a cross! These boards saved my life!" I was speechless. Not only was I astounded that Carl was not seriously hurt or even killed, but because he saw the cross as what saved him. Inwardly I was wildly thanking the Lord. This was a sign to me that my husband would soon be with me on this most interesting journey of faith in God. It would be another year.

CHAPTER 10

You Belong to Us!

My new tranquility was rudely interrupted one night when I woke up with a start to the presence of evil. It felt like an evil person had entered the room yet I saw no one else in the darkened room. Terror struck my heart, the hair on the back of my neck stood up. *"You belong to us"—"You were in our playground, you opened the doors and you belong to us now."* I was paralyzed with fear. The voice, whether inside of my head or outside, I couldn't tell, sounded intimidating. "Who are you? What are you?" I struggled to perceive what was going on. I felt as though I had been taken prisoner as I lay on my bed. Suddenly I heard my own voice. *"Jesussss!"* Still frozen, lying in my bed, the evil presence began to leave the room. I kept saying, *"Jesus help me."* Carl was snoring, oblivious to my distress. After quietness resumed, I fell back to sleep. The next night I was undisturbed. However, a few nights later, it happened again. This time I was completely paralyzed and could not speak out loud. It was like being pinned down in a dense spider web with no oxygen. I could not come to complete consciousness though I fought wildly to sit up and call for Jesus to help me. I could not do it. Finally I cried on the inside with all of my might: *"JESUS!"* Relief came again at the inner cry of HIS name! The paralysis left and I was able to move and speak again. Like Peter, James and John in the stormy sea that was quieted the moment Jesus said, "Peace, be still," they said, "Who is this who can calm the storm?" I said to myself, "Wow, who is this who has power over evil and dark beings?" But I knew. Jesus was proving to me who He really was—a truth I desperately needed to know. He had truly conquered the devil and was all-powerful.

As thankful as I was to know that Jesus was on high alert for my benefit, it was difficult not to be afraid to go to sleep at night. I began to be afraid of the experience of fear itself. The evil presence produced an atmosphere of stark terror. But the reality began to dawn on me. When I accepted Jesus into my life I had entered into a spiritual reality that I had not known before. Little did I know at the time but the real battle for my soul *had just begun.*

It took a considerable amount of time to understand that the New Age Movement and the occult practices were not just an amusement or the latest fad in the counter culture. It was a well-organized strategy to produce spiritual death in defenseless seekers who were bored with the status quo. This was a cleverly planned deception from the ages to a generation that would open their minds to what had *not been familiar.* Unseen malevolent forces were masquerading in the guise of New Age practices, seducing the generation of baby boomers. The age of enlightenment was a marquee for deception and the activity of fallen beings whose sole purpose was to thwart the plans of the true God and those who joined Him.

My eyes were opened the day I read chapter eighteen of the book of Deuteronomy in the Bible.

> *Deut. 18:10-14 There shall not be found among you any one that makes his son or*

> *his daughter to pass through the fire, or that uses divination, or an observer of times, or an enchanter, or a witch,*
> *Or a charmer, or a consulter with familiar spirits, or a wizard, or a necromancer. For all that do these things are an abomination unto the LORD: and because of these abominations the LORD thy God doth drive them out from before thee.*
> *Thou shalt be perfect with the LORD thy God.*
> *For these nations, which thou shalt possess, hearkened unto observers of times, and unto diviners: but as for thee, the LORD thy God hath not suffered thee so to do.*

I examined these verses that read like archaic prose. The definitions of these words sounded familiar somehow. I became arrested in my spirit. These words might be ancient but because they are from the Bible and they are *timeless.* A chill went down my spine. I sensed I was on the verge of a major revelation as I grappled with understanding what was happening in my life and *why?* I grabbed my study aids and began to dissect each word from the meaning of the word, even going back to the original Hebrew definition of the word. As I did, there before me were the very occult practices that had pulled me in so cleverly. Divination has to do with exactly what my psychic teacher, Claudia, practiced. She used a power that was not her own—neither was it from God. She told the futures of vulnerable, unsuspecting ones like myself. She was clear about her powers. She would speak to me of spirits by name as though they were great friends. She told me her psychic abilities came from spirits who had power beyond human limitations. They are cunning and know things beyond what the five senses could possibly know. When I saw in those Scriptures that these practices were *an abomination to the Lord,* it blew my mind! Upon facing the truth that these occult practices were an abomination to the Lord, I cried. I did those things! And it was evident to me that my ignorance of this truth did not protect me from suffering the consequences of my reckless behavior. The cover was being ripped off of the true nature of my distress. The Bible, the inspired word of the true God, had warned long ago of these New Age practices which were not new at all. The reason God proclaimed these magic arts to be an abomination is because they were initiated by false gods that led the people whom He loved so dearly into idolatry and ultimately to destruction. The reason for His vehement opposition was not because He is a divine task master with His fist raised, demanding exclusive rights to be worshiped. It is His love that created this warning because He knew the outcome.

He knew the pain and destruction that followed in the wake of this path. I can compare this reality to that of the law of gravity. Even if you knew nothing about gravity, and thought just maybe you could fly, and stepped off of a tall building, you would plummet to your untimely death. Whether or not you believed in the law of gravity would make no difference. Now I was beginning to know what sin was all about and that indeed I was a sinner. The light was dawning about my true guilt and why Jesus went to the cross. As I contemplated the love behind His actions for me, I was undone.

Despite the fact that I had become entangled in these deceptions, inside I was searching for the truth. Popular relativism was born in my generation, yet I had a driving desire to know the truth of what this world was really all about and if there is a divine and grand plan for all of us.

As my Bible search intensified, I saw other Scriptures

that seemed to be a part of the mystery. In the New Testament it is written as follows:

> *Eph 6:11-13 Put on the whole armor of God that ye may be able to stand against the wiles of the devil. For we wrestle not against flesh and blood, but against principalities, against powers, against the rulers of the darkness of this world, against spiritual wickedness in high places. Wherefore take unto you the whole armor of God that ye may be able to withstand in the evil day, and having done all, to stand.*

The Bible continued to provide information as to why my life had turned upside down. Who or what.... are these principalities, and dark rulers, evil beings mentioned here? The devil does not at all sound like a cartoon character with two horns and a forked tail. To be honest, I was spooked to the core when I first began to uncover these truths about the occult and New Age movement. I began to suspect that my deep depression and even the push to take my life was a planned strategy against me. I believe this plan was designed to rob me from my God and Creator who loves me more than words could say. He loved me so much that He had a divine plan to redeem me from the grip of death, and sin. Because of other immutable laws of the universe, similar to that of gravity, His own divine Son would have to shed His blood to cover sin and darkness and set us free from its cruel tyranny. His death on that tree reconciled us back to our loving Father. My Bible search brought me face to face with truth-and the truth was setting me free!

CHAPTER 11

A Long Haul

Two years after my turning point, I was beginning to be curious about the churches nearby. I loved my time with Jesus and me, but I realized that as a believer, I was swimming upstream in a raging river of people who did not believe in Jesus and were in fact hostile toward him. I no longer doubted God. I knew that what I now possessed was the key to life. I had wanted to know what truth was! Now I knew I had it, but it was costly. I had new desires and a growing dislike of my old ways. I hated smoking cigarettes. It wasn't long and the desire to quit smoking drove me to my knees. I still drank socially, but it was not a habit any longer. Neither was pot smoking. As my old vices fell away so did a lot of my friends. They soon knew that I was no longer 'one of them.' I continued to tag along with Carl, praying and hoping that he would join me in this most amazing Jesus journey.

There was a local church group I wanted to visit as they were known to have hippies in it. But as I was making my plans to attend a service, I had a quiet but distinct sense down inside that this was not the place for me. I was in a school of learning about how to hear God's voice and the ways in which He communicated to His children. As I waited for answers to my inquiries about which church to visit, a family

I was acquainted with through my job invited me to their church that was about fourteen miles away. I hesitated but had a definite peaceful feeling inside every time I thought about it. So I went to visit. The same peace was present and soon I was attending regularly.

Being in the presence of others who believed was a novelty. I was reserved but my confidence grew. I could sense the same presence of God when I was with this congregation that I had in the woods that day. It was not as strong, but it gave me comfort that I was among kindred spirits. I began to learn more of what was in the Bible and what it meant. My newest prayer was, *"Lord, I want everything you have for me!"* My ability to trust God was growing. I knew that He was only good and His mysterious ways could be trusted. I heard amazing things contained in the Bible that helped me re-program my thinking—at least in most areas.

It was quite difficult for me to retain the fact that God could really love *me*. I would sense it at times and recall my life-changing encounter, however, I seemed to end up in a pit of doubt about His love for *me*. The Bible confirmed this truth about His love. Why would He go through all that suffering if He didn't? My feelings were not just some little whimsical emotions fluttering in my soul. They were powerful surges that ran counter to everything else in my senses. The thought realm and feeling realm defied all that I wanted to believe and all that I read in the Bible. I could believe that love is for others. In fact I began to love those around me in a real way. When I had my own children, I was better able to understand love. But receiving love for myself seemed to be obstructed. Rumbling deep beneath the surface was a gnawing guilt and a feeling that I deserved only punishment.

My feelings of insecurity did not disappear even though I accepted the truth of forgiveness and love. At times, I would seem to be fighting unseen ghosts that tormented my thoughts and caused horrible feelings of doom. Each time this happened I would call to Jesus and each time I would find relief. It was like an unseen cloud of dimness that followed me. When the episodes were especially long, I would fling myself to my knees and call Jesus. His sweet presence would obliterate the turbulence and give me peace again. During one exceptionally long and difficult period, I felt I could take it no longer. I knelt down and buried my face in sobs of hopelessness. In this distraught state, I saw in a vision in my mind. Jesus was standing over me. He placed His hands on my head and said, "You are free from this now." I felt His presence. As my tears subsided and the warmth of His holy love ran into me, I heard a soft and high pitched song coming from my own lips. It was a song in a language I had never before heard. It came from the depth of my spirit as I sang and sang. Somehow I realized that I was singing in the 'other tongues' that are spoken of in the New Testament. I learned much later that when a person has opened the door to the powers of darkness through occultic practices, Satan will assign a spirit counselor to follow that person. When Jesus touched me that day, I felt He personally dismissed that dark cloud from my life. I was so happy. My hope returned and I was overjoyed that He came to me again. I soared in the heavenlies for quite a while after that. I hung onto His love for the longest time since receiving Him. If only I could keep it inside and not lose it now.

CHAPTER 12

New Horizons

In the fourth year of our marriage, I became pregnant. Carl and I had been using very risky birth control so we should not have been surprised. Although we had the top of our house framed in, we had not yet completed the main floor of our homemade log A-frame. We had become quite comfortable living downstairs in our walk-out capped basement. When we received the news, we put our building plans into high gear. We wanted to beat our baby's birthdate and be living upstairs by that time.

Pregnancy and I did not get along too well. The frequent nausea was the most problematic feature. When the second trimester rolled around and I began to feel movement, I was swept off my feet by my little invader. As many of my 'back to earth' contemporaries, I had a strong desire to have a natural childbirth. My newborn was not about to be influenced by pain drugs which could make him/her sluggish and inactive. I read everything I could get my hands on about the growing fetus, the birth, and the coming stages of development.

From the beginning I wanted a home birth. I loathed the sterile smelly hospital setting. Home births were gaining in popularity among the baby boomers. It made so much sense. Childbirth was not a disease, why should it take place in a hospital that is intended for sick individuals? I already possessed the pioneer spirit of my generation. I began to pray and plan. Now that my life belonged to Jesus, I made Him my chief consultant. Carl was a close second.

My doctor was the hippie doctor in town. He wore a single earring, and had lengthy locks long before it was fashionable. He had the persona of being half-stoned without a care in the world—traits all flower children admired. His wife at the time was a midwife. This brought a timely amount of encouragement and direction from people who I felt knew what they were doing!

The main house structure was not yet completed when the due date rolled along. However, the cute, hand- made A frame was closed in and dry. Since the bathroom was functioning, we put our antique oak bed upstairs, and determined it was a perfect place for the birth of our baby!

Three weeks after the due date came and went, I was laying in bed reading a novel, finally getting drowsy, when I heard a strange sound like a muffled but distinct "click". I wonder "What was that?" An unusual sound, indeed! A few moments later, when I shifted my heavy load to a more comfortable position, I felt a wet and warm sensation down under. *"Whaaaat?"* It took a few moments for me to realize what was happening. It was the amniotic fluid draining out from a burst placenta! Baby time! *"Carl. Wake up!"* I no sooner screamed for Carl to wake up when my first contraction came. *It was a ripsnorter!* Ow! I surely don't need to wonder any more what a contraction feels like and if I would recognize it to be a birth pang. We hustled, prepared and called the midwife to come. The contractions came on me like a speeding locomotive. I had practiced the breathing techniques known to help with the more painful contractions. I had a focal point that was a small window ornament of stained glass that resembled a sunset. It was so pretty, so perfect, so me. But before the birth of our son, 12 hours later, this ornament took on the characteristics of a mini monster face. My labor was fierce and threatened to overwhelm me at times. I worked hard to breathe the correct patterns I had learned. Carl was with me all the way, coaching and loving me. The miracle of birth became a reality and my handsome and healthy son emerged, screaming appropriately, needing his mommy to comfort and nurse him. We named our seven and one half pound bundle of joy Sean Joseph. The feelings at that moment were pure ecstasy and worth all of the labor pain. The powerful maternal hormones released into sobs and tears of relief. A sense of rapture filled the room with a soft glow as we beheld a true miracle of creation. For the next three days, I floated in the heights of heaven as I fell more in love with my baby boy. The previous two years of battling to escape the darkness of my past, made this time all the more wonderful, full of love, and abundant hope for myself.

Carl was a very good daddy. He did not shy away from changing stinky cheesy diapers. Being a daddy brought out the tender side of this tough Marine. He would sit holding the baby and just gaze at this tiny miracle. Tears would well up in his eyes every time. The quality of his love would soon be tested as baby Sean formed an attachment of preference with mommy. Nursing creates a strong bond for obvious reasons. But even when hungry baby Sean was screaming for mommy, Carl's love was stronger than any feelings of personal rejection. His unconditional love and joy for his son, and later for his daughters, produced a rewarding relationship in the years to follow. He just had to wait a little.

Two more children graced our lives over the next seven years. Gorgeous Holly, with a full head of dark hair, emerged two and a half years after Sean was born. We enjoyed a perfect home birth in the bedroom loft of our not-yet-finished log A-frame. Holly Sue was a joy beyond words. She was strong willed but so very affectionate. Her dark locks turned into roots of pure blonde when she was nine months old. Weren't we surprised?

Five years afterward, Shari Ann, so tiny and delicate, came into our lives. She was even more strong-willed than her sister. Shari did not waste any time displaying her emerging talents and was singing her own songs at an early age. Shari was born in the local hospital due to a potential complication. It was at this time I was forced to deal with childhood trauma that resulted from an experience when I was six years old. Though I had boasted of being a pioneer in the home birth arena, the truth was I was terrified of hospitals. I had been very sick and hospitalized at a children's hospital in Milwaukee. The medical staff had never seen this before in a young child, but diagnosed me with mononucleosis. I had crabby nurses, and was tied down in the hospital bed because of all of my screaming. They would not let my parents in to see me at first because they thought my illness could be infectious. There were other unfortunate situations that all added up to permanent damage to the emotions of a first grader. When it became necessary for me to be in the hospital for the birth of my baby, I began to steel myself and I prayed.

My third birth was difficult—for both Shari and I. But thankfully, she was born in good health. The nurses who attended my beautiful baby daughter and myself were nothing short of angelic. They were so comforting and reassuring, I soon forgot those difficulties and began to enjoy my baby girl. More healing came to me as I continued in my life of faith.

My children were my delights in the midst of those stormy years when the past continued to nip at my heels.

There were still times when I would experience debilitating fear and anxiety. But healing and deliverance became a way of life for me. Every event seemed to produce healing in one form or another. This was good. But I didn't realize how extensive my former life style had impaired me. Nor could I have known that that real liberation was still before me. This phase of life as a young mother was crucial for the future as I was discovering who I was. The God of Grace was giving me a life that I could call my own and was showing me that life was intended to be good.

Carl and I were quite busy being parents and working as well. I owned and operated a day care center. I had put my administrative gifts to use applying for state startup funds. I received $7,000 to start my town's first day care center. I made use of my child development education and produced a preschool program that the parents loved. I was happy with the success of this venture.

Little Sean was going on one year when the baby sitter witnessed his first steps. The new me, with bundles of love for my child, wanted to see my baby's first step! I wanted to be there with him. I did *not* want to hear about his milestones from the babysitter! My disappointment turned to distress. It was time to go to the big boss. I took a half day off from work to pray. Why did I think that working was the right thing to be doing? As I lay stretched crossways on my bed, pouring out my heart to the Lord, I distinctly heard, *"Sell your business and come home."* It was so clear. I began to ponder this possibility and before I knew what I was doing I was dancing and laughing in my kitchen. As I thought about selling the day care center, a plan of action occurred to me. My joy shot off the chart! I could hardly wait to see Carl. If he agreed this plan was a good one, I would put it into action immediately. I knew he would likely support my decision even if he didn't like the fact that our income would be reduced. To my relief, Carl concurred with the plan one hundred percent.

Together we agreed that we would raise our own children no matter what the cost. We would not relegate this holy trust to a babysitter or a day care center, even the one I so carefully created. We discussed ways we could save money and decided together that my plan should be put in motion. Amazingly, in three short weeks, my business was sold to a reliable buyer and I was home with my darling baby. I couldn't have been happier. I did vow to myself, however, that I would not be the stereotypical 'Suzie Homemaker.' I would make our nest. I would take time for what was important in a way that was uniquely and creatively my own.

I was very content to be home but a negative side to this lifestyle was that I had far too much time to think. I would be home alone with Sean with no one else to talk to. I made strong attempts to discipline my mind and thoughts, but at odd moments I would hear a diatribe that was fearful and foreboding. I feared bad things happening. I feared something happening to my baby, my husband, myself. Driving to town began to throw me into anxiety. I cried out to the Lord as I always did. Even though I did not experience His presence as I had in the past during difficult times, I felt prodded to open the Bible during these times. Amazingly, every time I did, I found myself reading the exact passages that I needed to be encouraged.

Jeremiah 30:5 *"Cries are heard, cries of fear and not of peace"* You hear me, O Lord, you really hear my cries for help. I began to write down scriptures on 3x5 cards. I would take them with me wherever I went. There were times that I could not drive to town without reading the Bible verses over and over again to gain the courage I needed to face the enemy within myself.

After making an appointment with the pastor of the

church I attended, I sat in front of him, in his office. I told him of my woes. He had already prayed for me a number of times. He showed that he cared about my situation, but he expressed that he did not really know how to help me at this point. He recommended that I visit a church that was located about an hour or so to the south. He said there was a lot of Holy Spirit activity going on there. He suggested that I go visit and take along another woman from the church who was also having a difficult time.

Two weeks later, I was zooming down the freeway with a new friend in the passenger seat. Her name was Sondra. Little did we know at the time, but we would become close friends as we traveled to this Holy Spirit church many times in the years to come. We were pursuing freedom and chasing after God. The investment paid off, but it would take some time.

CHAPTER 13

Deliverance

Carl was becoming accustomed to the Friday night routine. I would drive 80 miles to the church service and he would be with the children. He was supportive most of the time. He wanted me to get the help I needed. Carl had received Jesus into his life about two years earlier. His salvation experience was far less dramatic but no less true. We both were slowly changing into conscientious adults with a new paradigm. Our world view was now centered on the true God who so loves the world that He sent His only begotten Son, Jesus Christ, who intervened and transformed our lives. One of the most dramatic revelations that changed our lives was the awareness of the spiritual battle. The sixth chapter of the book of Ephesians quoted earlier describes a 'war in the heavenlies' that is chilling. The need for me to become very familiar with these verses was evident. I could almost see these fallen beings more wicked, ugly and foreboding than any monsters or dragons Hollywood could produce on the big screen!

God's love for me gave me the courage to face the facts about what I had gotten involved with. God's love for me was so great that He led me on this amazing journey of discovery so that I could be completely released from the darkness that tried to destroy me. One of the facts I had to face was that the spirit guides I was introduced to in the New Age movement were not at all who I was told they were. I was taught that these were friendly spirits who could help humans. Supposedly they were part of what was called the 'universal consciousness' and could impart knowledge and personal power. People who begin to practice New Age activities will eventually receive these guides in one form or another. Most people start out by experimenting with things like horoscopes, healing and relaxation techniques, transcendental meditation, and yoga, but soon go deeper into an exploration of the supernatural and quests for secret knowledge and the attainment of 'god within.' With each new practice a person becomes more entrenched. The spirit guides will subtly lead the seeker into greater depths of deception. These practices can feel very spiritual and even exciting, as though you have found secrets of life that others do not know about. Little did I know that these were the 'beings' the Bible says were sent to prevent me from finding the real truth about life and death, heaven and hell and the true holy God. Through my spiritual rebirth that the Bible tells about, I understood these beings were fallen from heaven along with Satan, and everything began to make sense to me. Now I understood that these forces were not friendly spirit guides to help humans, but rather were imposters counterfeiting the real spiritual power that belongs to God alone. They are invisible forces working behind the scenes to influence people using deception—producing a level of power in an attempt to counterfeit the true power that comes from the Holy Spirit. As a new believer, my eyes were being opened. I *had* to learn the truth, because it is the TRUTH that sets us free.

What was unfolding before my eyes was the greatest love story ever told—the love story of God whose creation went into darkness but was rescued by the Creator Himself. The age old argument from the atheist corner that 'if there is a God, why is there all this evil in the world,' is quite pathetic. For me, it is not difficult to believe that a good and powerful God made His creation to be like Him as free moral agents who had the ability to choose Him or the evil. I am quite sure He did not want a bunch of robotic beings who had no ability to know anything *but Him*. He allowed the perfect storm so His best created beings--humans, made in His image, could achieve family status by, of all things, *trusting Him, believing in the Son He sent.* He brought the perfect solution in a world that could never perform or compete well enough to win Him through human ingenuity or strength. He made a level playing field. He gave us the stars to behold, in addition to the majesty of planet earth. The incredible beauty and magnitude of the stars alone give any person pause to wonder about creation and stirs the 'inner knowing' that a powerful creator exists. But even more incredible and stunning is the truth that we can know Him in a personal way. I grew up in church *and never knew HIM!* I thought God was an angry God who spied on you to catch you in sin and then shamed you for being human. I did not know who He really was and that He loved me and sent His Son to fix things so He could have me back. It is unfathomable. This is the ultimate love story—quite staggering to the finite mind. The 'Good News' is about a passionate God who would not allow us to be snatched away from Him. The war against my destiny had been waging since I was conceived. The worst, most precarious and painful time of my life led me to a living relationship with the most amazing being I have ever known. He knew all along that one day I would call for help.

When Sondra and I entered the church building called Valley Chapel, I was enraptured with the tangible presence of love. It was palpable. This presence of God's love was like coming home. It was this presence that entered my crazily spinning world just a few years ago. It was like I could breathe again. As I began to enter into the singing and praising, I was touched by the humility of those doing the singing. The ones who spoke were also down to earth, and very authentic in all they said. I wanted to be like these people. They had love for others. They had love for me even though they did not know me, at least not yet. It was in this environment that I received another revolutionary truth that not only impacted my world, *but would set me apart from many in the church world for the rest of my life.*

Once the people at Valley Chapel had become acquainted with me and my past, they formed a strategy for prayer on my behalf. They seemed to understand much about the ramifications of occult involvement and how it affects a person. This was reassuring and in contrast to those who were intimidated by my past and even afraid to pray for me. This gave me confidence and hope.

It was on the third visit that the couple who prayed with me addressed the sins of my past. They helped me understand to an even greater degree the consequence of involvement with the New Age movement and the occult. Yes, I was forgiven. I had turned completely away from these practices and also *renounced* my involvement. I began to see that complete victory was not automatic but needed to be won over time, one right choice at a time. As I continued learning on this spiritual battlefield, I began to become more proficient at wielding the weapons I needed to fight and win! This was exactly what was meant in the Scriptures by "overcoming." I could only do it through a right relationship with God and with a knowledge of His truths as revealed in His Word. It had not been easy so far and I did not know what this next battle would be like.

As we continued in prayer sitting in our small circle in a quiet corner of the sanctuary, one of the people began to speak to the spirits of the occult directly. I had received prayer at my home church, but this was a different approach. As things became quiet, I began to rise from my chair. I assumed we were finished and I would soon be driving home. But what happened next, nothing could have prepared me for. Through no decision or action of my own, strange sounding laughter came from my lips. It sounded like a witch cackling! The people praying spoke to the spirits and commanded that they leave me because I now belonged to Jesus. They said, "In the name of Jesus you must leave her." The strange laugh was in reality the spirit manifesting its nature. As they spoke the command again, it was like the old fashioned 'jack in the box' toy. As you turned the little crank, the lid opened and out popped the spring-loaded surprise! Something rushed out of my mouth in screams. They continued calmly to pray in English and in their heavenly language. By the time they were done, I was weeping—tears of hope and relief streamed down my face. In addition to this astounding relief, I could feel love through these wonderful people who laid down their lives and schedules to help set me free. Something like a warm glow rushed into my inner person and I knew it was God's holy love. I felt so cherished and loved…and clean!

This experience opened my eyes even more to the realities of the spiritual world while integrating them with the three dimensional here and now. Jesus had heard my cries. He penetrated my world and changed my reality. I was falling madly in love with Him. My faith was not some religious exercise or dead form. So, this is what the Good News was really all about!

New levels of hope filled my life. I had a clear understanding now that my deliverance is a process as my faith grew. Jesus would continue to set me free but it would only be as I grew up in Him and could stand my ground in the truth and not go back to the old ways, even in my thinking. It was about learning to trust Him in all things—including trusting Him and overcoming all of the fear and brokenness *that took me into the occult in the first place.*

Facing the fact that the devil is a real force in the modern world took a little time and faith. This reality frightened me considerably. It seemed the devil was directly responsible for the terrible depressive and fearful feelings by playing upon my past sin and ignorance. He was defeated when Jesus endured the cross and rose from the grave. But I had given him a legal right to access my life when I practiced what the Bible warned us not to do. Now, I knew the truth. But it was just as true that these very battles are what made my faith grow strong and rooted in the love God has for me. All of this put me in a position to have to lean on the Lord and trust Him. Little by little I overcame. I had heard the Lord say to me during one of my many battles, *"Do not fear the enemy attacks, for they are stepping stones for you."* I immediately understood what He meant. There was no escape from the battles but I was reassured that He would help me and make me stronger and freer with each one.

As I continued to be renewed in my mind and soul, a new gift emerged in my life—music. I began to sing and play the guitar. A passion for music, along with musical ability, was in my DNA. My mother possessed a beautiful soprano voice and played piano. My father played numerous musical instruments—guitar, piano, harmonica, and accordion. I had taken piano lessons for a few years and although I was not proficient, I enjoyed playing and singing. I had an instrument that replicated an auto harp, however it was electronic, utilizing technology to produce the sounds of a harp. It was easy to play and accompany myself with. I began to write songs that just seemed to pour out of my spirit. Some of these songs would bring healing to others. This was a great joy for me.

Singing songs of praise and worship took on an important role in my restoration. As I would release myself in song and pour out my love to God, I learned I was able to perceive the difference between my heart (emotions, will, intellect) and my spirit which is the place where the Holy Spirit dwells in me. The frequent battles which pulled me down into depressive states were alleviated when I would sing praises to the Lord. The act of singing lifted me up into a realm of faith, hope, and love. The ability to differentiate these parts of my being was valuable. Many mornings I would feel a cloud of heaviness on my emotions. This negative feeling would tempt me to doubt in all of the healing and restoration that God had provided. Why couldn't I wake up happy? I was happy in the literal sense but this heavy feeling caused me to think I was not. I had to thoroughly learn the difficult lesson that feelings are fickle and not to be trusted. As I learned how to tend to my own soul, I discovered that when I started my day singing to the Lord, I was lifted out of the grey cloud.

Valley Chapel continued to be a regular destination for several years. It seemed that this work of deliverance was engineered in a very specific way by the Holy Spirit. As each area would rise to the surface, triggered by various events in my life, I would do the work of examining the lies I had believed in my former life and replacing them with the truth of God's Word. As I stood my ground when Satan attacked my mind, I would become strong. Ultimately I would receive prayer with my faithful prayer partners and more demons would be cast out of my soul. With each battle, I would see my Savior more clearly and receive more of His love and grace.

Although it seems bizarre to our natural minds, through the deliverance ministry, the Lord was exposing the true enemy of my soul. He guided me every step of the way. My ability to trust the Lord and know His secure love skyrocketed. This was not *religious form*, which lacks power. What I experienced was the true Gospel which *has* power. For a soul imprisoned to be healed and delivered is a miracle. Our Savior is all powerful and all loving. He came to my rescue and set me free. The battle was worth it all.

CHAPTER 14

Persecution and Rejection from the Church

My years of deliverance and restoration were shrouded with whirlwinds of persecution and rejection from the church world. My prolonged season of restoration became an enigma to many church leaders who were unfamiliar with the dynamics of occult bondage. They did not seem to understand that the captivity of the soul of a person to dark powers required a *process* in order to successfully and thoroughly extricate them from this horrible web. They thought that a few prayers from the leaders should do the trick and bring conformity to the rest of the Body of Christ.

During the first phase of my life as a believer, I needed constant reassurance as I could not hold on to this love for any length of time yet. Slowly and methodically the Lord healed me and empowered me to know beyond a shadow of a doubt that I could trust in His love for me personally in any and every situation life could throw at me!

As months turned into years and I was continuing to experience restoration, I began to talk about it to others. Some of my friends grasped what was going on, being happy that the Spirit of God was working so powerfully in my life. Some of the people did not understand and were agitated by my story. My testimony of being set free from demonic spirits was disturbing to those who had no teaching in this regard. Many saw my life as a roller coaster and indeed, it was for quite some time. Yet for those who knew me well, it was obvious that I was changing for the better with each valley and height I experienced. People came to me years later and confessed how uncomfortable it made them to see me going to the altar again and again, weeping and broken. They wanted to discount me as a hopeless case, and dismiss me as a failure. But in the course of time, they began to see the transformation of my life. They saw me as a compassionate and radical believer who could not only stand, but take down the darkness as well. One lady was terrified of the very personal transparency she saw displayed in me, yet at the same time she saw something wonderful that was out of her grasp. *"How can you love so much? I don't have that kind of love for others."* Those moments gave me valuable opportunities to forgive my persecutors and encourage them to also let the inner work of the Spirit take place in their own souls. I began to understand that when we are truly following Jesus, it is not that opposition may come, *it will come,* and we must be prepared to forgive and love like Jesus did.

For years I prayed for others to be set free like I had been. I discovered that one did not need to have been involved in occultism to have a need for deliverance and restoration. There are many areas of our soul and emotions that can be damaged and controlled by darkness rather than love. There can be areas of unforgiveness, bitterness, rejection, rebellion and many more areas that need the delivering power of Jesus. Deliverance is not the answer for everything, *but what deliverance does, nothing else can do.* It is the power of the gospel to bring transformation in the areas of our lives that often gives us the most trouble.

Due to a lack of understanding, local people were afraid of me. This fear prompted people to gossip about me. This led to more talk and then rumors. They had heard the rumors that I had the 'devil's power.' One woman said she was afraid to talk to me. Another told me years later that what had been said about me would take her 'years to get over.' Unfortunately some of the local pastors, most of whom did not even know me, joined in the chatter about the 'woman who had been in the occult,' spread the mistrust toward me, and inadvertently fueled the gossip. If they would have taken the time to get to know me and the truth about my path of restoration, they could have been a support instead of a hindrance. It hurt deeply to be rejected in this way. An elderly retired pastor named George and his wife Ethel were prayer partners with me at the time. They played a key role in encouraging me during those turbulent days. George attended some of the pastors' prayer meetings and heard with his own ears the negative talk about me. He told me about it and with a hearty laugh said, "Don't worry, I know you, *the real you.*"

In all of my days of difficult spiritual warfare, I was tempted sorely by the devil to doubt and deny Jesus. He would torment me and try to wear me down, even tempting me to return to old powers and old ways, but I never did. I was always growing stronger spiritually no matter what I may have looked like on the outside. One day coming out of church on a Sunday, a woman approached me without a smile. She said in a stern manner, "Where is your joy?" I felt the sting of unspoken criticism immediately, though the irony of her less-than-joyful approach should have been amusing. True, I did not look very joyful most of the time back then. It was work to stay on top of the battle that was riddled with depressing moments and overwhelming pressures. I responded to this woman before I could think too much about the impact of my words: *"My joy is that I did not curse God and die today. I have never denied Jesus in all of the devil's attempts to destroy my life. I have hung on to Him with all of my might."*

The firestorm of accusation and rejection played a crucial role in my spiritual development. All of this opposition was producing in me a foundation of faith so that my trust was not in people, or leaders, but in God alone. As painful as it all was, these experiences brought me even closer to God and helped me to cling to His love and acceptance of me. I have forgiven my persecutors. Jesus taught us how to do this. It is a must if we want to walk in freedom.

My own pastor, who had the love and wisdom to send me to specialists in another church, had questions too. For a time he fell prey to the attack against me. He said things to us and others that cut deeply into my already wounded soul. It was a difficult time for me. I felt so defeated. Sure I had plenty of flaws I couldn't hide. But I was getting better and freer all the time. The dark spirits that hovered over me screamed at me that I would *always be a problem.* I felt like a hopeless case. The misunderstanding reached critical mass. Carl and I and our three children left the church.

The day came and the Lord vindicated me to my pastor. Together we triumphed over this savage attack against all of us. Carl and I had precious reconciliation with him. A few years later, we returned to the church and enjoyed a new level of acceptance and love there. The people in the congregation realized that rumors were false. We were all tested in one sense. For us it was to truly forgive from the heart, and for them it was to release the judgements many had made. There were times I could literally feel my Father God's delight that we had returned and were restored.

The battle is real as well as painful. It exposes the hidden roots of our soul that are naturally hateful and bitter. Yet these conflicts and trials are the tools God uses to transform us on the inside. When we forgive, we are changed.

When we love rather than self-protect, we are walking in the footsteps of Jesus.

Today, this same pastor, now retired, cheers me on in all the Lord has given me to do for His kingdom. He is the kind of man who overcomes evil with good. His example has helped many others in ministry. When we triumph over the enemy together, our relationships become stronger than before. This is what the God-kind-of-love is all about.

During the time of church tensions, Carl and I thought we should try a different church. We knew the importance of staying connected to the Body of believers. The second week we attended the new church, I decided to go to the evening service. It was a smaller group who gathered to sing and pray for one another. Although I was feeling very fearful that these people would also reject me, at the same time I was cautiously hopeful that perhaps we would fit in here. I felt the soft glow of God in the atmosphere. The service was almost over when the pastor invited all to come up front and form a circle, joining hands to pray. As people ventured out in prayer, I saw the simple faith of the people and felt comfort. Without advance notice I began to cry. The soft sound quickly escalated to an audible sobbing. My chest heaved as loud weeping filled the room. All fell silent as the dam broke and all of the rejection of the past several years flooded to the surface. I didn't know what to do. My sobbing was out of control and I couldn't stop it though I tried. The pastor sized up the situation quickly and said in a tender voice, "We have a broken heart here, people. Let's pray for our sister." Softly the small group prayed. I felt no judgement, only love. I would not know for several years that this man and his wife, Gary and Lorraine, would play a key role in my future across the Atlantic Ocean.

One of the redeeming features of these transitional years for Carl and I was a series of home meetings that we hosted in the remote corner of our north woods. The Lord sent a very special shepherd into our life from the neighboring state. Remi came right into our home and provided us with fresh manna. We would have a time of praise and worship and then he would preach to us. He always preached about the cross, helping us to receive all that had been accomplished for us. We would invite others who were hurting. This man would pray and help us receive from the Lord. His humble and very honest ways were refreshing. He possessed a wonderful prophetic gift. This gift would build us up in our faith.

Our home became like a spiritual hospital for those who were bleeding and rejected. People who were on God's kind of life support were healed—their hope and faith renewed. At one point, during a time of prayer, Remi saw a mental picture of me as a lamb with broken legs from the battering of the shepherd's rods. Many tears flowed during that time and much healing came, not only to me but to Carl and others who would come to join us. Many had been hurt in various church situations. All felt like outcasts. They would not enter a church building, but they would come into our home, a safe place.

As the Lord continued to open up areas of hurt and bondage to be healed in my heart, I will never forget the day I saw Father God, in a vision, rise from His throne in heaven, and come to hold me in His arms. On that particular evening I was sitting glumly on a chair in the semi-circle of chairs in our living room. My chest was feeling like chopped up meat as the past feelings of desolation surfaced. Remi came over and sat next to me, took my arm and began to tell me again about the love of our Father for me. As he prayed for me to receive the substance of our Father's love, a warm electric-like charge went deep inside as I saw the vision. God cares so much that He would raise up from His eternal throne and come to meet me in my level of pain and trauma. It was too much. God's love overwhelmed me. God used this man, who also had known deep trauma and inner pain in his life, in a precious way to bring yet another healing from the emotional abandonment I had experienced as a child.

As our children grew and became school age we discovered a Christian school within driving distance. Operating the school was a small group of believers who were in Gordon, Wisconsin, about 40 miles north of us. We decided to enroll our son and daughter there. Sean was in the first grade. Holly was just in preschool. The intimacy of this group was a breath of fresh air. Many of the adults involved and the children had endured difficult lives and had many problems. But they had all discovered Jesus and were walking out their new lives in Him. Ron and Chris were the couple who pastored this lively flock. We felt at home with them. We also decided I should volunteer at the school. For me this was a time of practicing all I had been learning as a believer. I began to notice that my capacity to love others was growing stronger. Because people in this group were not pretentious, their 'stuff' hung out, yet they were able to love and accept each other in such an honest way. During this time we made lifelong friends.

When I was invited to teach the first graders at the Christian school to read, I jumped at the chance. There were nine children, including our son, who were in the small class. A few of the kids had learning disabilities and a few others had been victims of sexual and physical abuse from step parents. Most of the children had already experienced severe blows for their young ages.

One morning as I prepared to start our reading class, I felt a distinct nudging from the Holy Spirit, and then I heard Him speak to me: "Before you begin the lesson, play and sing the new song you brought about Father's love."

"God cares about you in each and every way.
God cares about you in all you do and say.
He is here to meet your need just come to Him and pray.
God cares about you in each and every way."

As I played my instrument and the children sang, it was clear that the Holy Spirit was up to something special. The children loved the song and wanted to keep singing it again and again. The tangible presence of God came into the classroom. Soon most of the children were laying on the floor weeping. Clearly Jesus was here and touching the broken places in these innocents. As I continued to sing, pray and watch, I observed how one child would wrap their arm over one and then another and begin to pray for them. The sight of the children praying for each other and comforting one another was deeply moving. After an hour the soft weeping subsided and joy came in its place. Now we were all hugging, smiling, and laughing. This was a precious time that once again revealed the tender loving care of our Shepherd for His lambs.

CHAPTER 15

Life Can Begin at Forty

The life I was now living was truly full. Carl and I were raising three great kids which brought a daunting yet marvelous challenge we had not yet experienced. Watching our children grow up was one of my great comforts. Sean was strong and athletic. He could run like a deer. He also possessed an uncanny sense of justice. He stood up to bullies in school and on the bus. He even had to suffer disciplinary action because he fought off a bully defending a smaller boy. His integrity was inspiring. One day when he was still so small, I heard a scream from the bedroom. Sean had seen a big, nasty bug land on Holly's arm. The bug was frightening to look at but he charged over and flung it off of his little sister. This kind of courage is part of Sean's personality. Holly was beautiful and sensitive as she grew up. We realized early on that she is also brilliant. She has a magnetic personality and to this day her smile can change the world. Shari Ann came along five years after Holly. I was delighted! Shari was born with a strong will and could 'stand her ground' against the older two. She also possessed an exceptional singing voice. She would sing new songs from the time she was five years old. All three of our children have musical talent and beautiful voices. To this day one of my chief joys is to hear them sing together with their delightful harmonies. Raising kids is filled with joys—tears, too, as any parent will confirm. We were learning how to lean on Jesus.

As I was approaching my 40th birthday, I found myself feeling down. When I stopped to contemplate my feelings, I realized there was good reason for my dejection. I had barely begun to live life and now I would be old—over the hill—onward to old age. Though this thinking was ridiculous, this is what I felt. All the years of restoration had truly given me a new life. I wanted to live now. Tragically, I thought turning 40 meant one had to become more responsible in life—one had to 'grow up.' I had missed many years of enjoying life because of the error of my ways. Now I had succumbed to the cultural stereotypical ideas about age. I felt really discouraged about my upcoming birthday.

There was, however, a big birthday present waiting for me directly from the Lord. Remi was our pastor at that time and was about to embark on a mission trip to Romania. He had been there previously and knew of the many opportunities there to share the gospel. He wanted to take a small team with him. Two years had passed after the revolution and the fall of the dictator there. The whole world had awakened to the plight of the Romanian people who lived under a repressive communist dictator, Nicolai Ceausescu, for 20 years. Remi requested that Carl and I consider the possibility of me accompanying him and the others to Romania for this two-week mission outreach.

Carl and I both felt the stirring of the Holy Spirit that I should go to Romania. Our children were old enough now to be without their mom for a short time. I was thrilled and terrified at the same time. The idea of flying in an airplane over the ocean is something that I did not relish. I did not fear flying in a transatlantic jet, but crashing into the ocean was a different matter to consider. Fear of drowning was something that had plagued me from childhood. But my life was all about overcoming my past, so what was I worried about? It is not like I would be going alone. I knew deep down that God was calling me to go to Romania. A few weeks later while driving, at a moment of tormenting doubt about this trip, I moaned out loud, *"Lord, why can't I just go to my neighbors with the good news, why must I travel thousands of miles away to do this?"* No sooner had I uttered these words, than a song came on the car radio with lyrics I will never forget. "<u>Take My love to the nations, tell them of My love for them.</u>" I pulled over on that lonely country road. The presence of God overshadowed me and I began to sob. The Holy Spirit whispered to me, "The Romanian people are ready for My love because of what they have endured for the last twenty years. Will you go?"

No sooner had I resolved to make this trip when I received a call from Remi saying he couldn't go. A situation came up that prevented him from being able to carry out his plan. The other people too had backed out of going to Romania for various valid reasons. I was disappointed and relieved at the same time. I could not tell which emotion was stronger, but felt it was out of my hands. That is until I heard this small but unmistakable inner voice of love say, *"Will you still go? Will you go and trust Me to take care of you?"* Inside I began to scramble and attempt to dismiss this as my own thoughts or some wild random thought from space. However, the voice of the Lord continued, *"You may select anyone you want to go with you and I will make the way."* This was a clear mandate. The Lord knew my faith was ready for this challenge and he was giving me instruction. A surge of excitement and raw faith spiked inside of me. I began to mentally scan my Christian brothers and sisters as I mulled over this notion of whom I would like to accompany me. It had to be someone who knew the realities of spiritual warfare who could be a profitable prayer partner on such a trip. This someone should really have international travel experience since I did not possess this valuable skill. Lila!

It had to be Lila, from the Gordon fellowship. She had become a dear friend who was a veteran believer. She had been through much and triumphed in her life, plus she had already been on an international assignment from the Lord. I loved her and I knew she loved me. It had to be her. "But Lord, she has a big family, it seems impossible that she could drop everything to go with me!" I pined inside, already plummeting when I thought of the remoteness of this idea becoming reality. Throwing aside the doubts, I knew that when God said something He really meant it. I grabbed the phone and called Lila. I spilled out my request and together we prayed over the phone. I felt the warm presence of the Lord building as we prayed. Before we hung up, we both knew that we had been summoned by the King.

Not in my wildest imagination would I have thought I would be flying to a foreign land, not knowing where I was going nor with whom I would be staying. When Pastor Jon, the main contact in Bucharest, Romania, found out I would be coming without my pastor, he tried to convince me *not* to come. He said it was dangerous in Romania and that I may not be equipped to handle the life there. I was offended. Jesus told me to go the Romanians. How could he question me when it was the Lord sending me? With a racing pulse, I assured him I was coming no matter what. When I hung up the phone, I noticed my hands trembling.

We were aware of the critical need for medical supplies in this stricken land. Romania had been devastated by the abuse of their cruel dictator. Families and farms had been destroyed. The farmers and their families were herded like livestock into the cities and forced to live in high rise apartments without jobs or sufficient food. Many of the formerly romantic and robust Romanian people became ill and depressed. The national finances were used to fund elaborate palaces for the communist elite and to build military forces. The women were forced to have babies that would be raised up to be the soldiers for this wicked man. The people became so poor they could not feed their children and began to abandon them to state orphanages where they languished in rooms full of cribs, neglected and malnourished.

The idea came to me to locate as many quality medications as we could here in the US so that we could hand carry these to the few doctors we knew about in Romania. It seemed like a proverbial drop in the ocean of need, but didn't Jesus bless a little boy's offering of two fish and five loaves and feed 5,000 hungry people? I began to call all kinds of pharmaceutical sales reps to ask about donations to a good cause. I stressed that the medicine could not be beyond its expiration date. Our family physician, who was an obstetrician and had Romanian heritage, agreed to help me. He was needed to sign for the medications and prepare a document of authorization which would be required by the authorities to pass as I traveled through the various customs checkpoints.

Lila and I continued to coordinate our trip details. We had to reduce the packaging of the meds to its simplest form in order to fit them all in our giant suitcase. The medicines we were planning to bring were like gold. Our donations included some of the latest and most efficacious antibiotics known in medicine. I was also bringing my musical instrument along to be able to minister songs that I had written wherever the door may open. I had been rehearsing simple phrases of the Romanian language.

My first trip was indeed a mission trip. It was a mission to learn how to trust the Lord, how to hear His leading in difficulties and also how to share his most attractive love to those who needed it most. It was also a major exercise in overcoming paralyzing fear and seeing the faithfulness of the One who said "Go!"

The two doctors who received most of our medicines and supplies were a married couple. They wept openly when they saw what we brought. They told us of how their hearts would break over and over when they had no way to treat those who were sick and in pain. There was one more physician we wanted to deliver some of the medications to. He was located in a hospital. When we finally found the place, we were ushered all over the building in attempts to locate this doctor. This was not the kind of hospital that I would have wanted to be in if I were ill. It looked to be one hundred years old. The awful combination of cheap antiseptic and body wastes made me nauseous. The metal beds were old, with green paint chipped off in many places. The hospital staff, which were few, did not smile and the air was filled with something that made you want to run for your life. The doctor was finally located and he received our gifts with thanks. *"Lila, let's get out of here!"* I whispered in her ear.

For Lila and myself, the time spent in Romania was nothing short of miraculous. It was filled with dangers, challenges, and triumphs. Before we even crossed the border from Hungary to Romania, we were in potential danger on the night train. We had been told by Pastor Jon, our contact in Bucharest, "Whatever you do, do not take the night train to Romania. There are thieves and murderers who gas the train cars and pillage the possessions and cash of the passengers." However, we were forced to take the night train, when we were delayed by authorities and told that we needed to get a visa in Budapest. This required an additional stay that was not on our itinerary. After waiting in line for several hours, we obtained the proper visa and then had to spend the night in Budapest. We stayed in a hotel that was supposedly a YMCA, but it was old and kind of musty smelling. The bathroom was down the hall from the bedroom. When we placed the key in the door, it was apparent that the lock had been damaged as well as the door. It appeared to have been hastily repaired. Lila and I noticed this at the same time and snapped our heads around to the other. "Protect us, Oh Lord," we said out loud.

We settled into our dingy room for the night, but before I could fall asleep I had a horrible feeling of terror come over my body. It was paralyzing and gave me the feeling of losing control of my mental faculties. I wanted to get up and go home. This feeling, like I was about to go crazy, was intolerable. I called to Lila to pray. We put into practice every weapon of spiritual warfare that we had ever known. I even got up to dance in worship before the Lord to break this mortifying spell. For hours, we waged war, and finally exhausted, Lila held me as I fell asleep. We woke up in the morning and left as soon as we could. It was not until months after we were home that it was shown to me by the Holy Spirit that we had been visited by a prince of darkness who tried to turn us back from our destination.

When we boarded the next train to Budapest, the night train, we were unaware of the hostilities between the Hungarians and the Romanians at that time. As we beat back the words of warning that night trains could be filled with theft and even murder, the tension put me over into a humorous mood. *"Lila, do you realize that because we had to wait for a visa, we have been thrown off our schedule? Not only are we riding the scary night train, but nobody in the whole world knows where we are right now!"* This struck my funny bone, Lila's too and we laughed out loud until tears rolled down our cheeks.

After a few hours of riding the rails, the train screeched to a halt. "Where are we?" I wondered quietly. After about 20 minutes of silence I heard shouting and looked out the window to see men with rifles and a big dog running on the walkway. In another moment they boarded our train and three of these soldiers or police, I was not sure, burst into our car, German shepherd and all. I was quite sure that all this drama was intended to intimidate us and *it was working!* The one man who spoke a little English asked for our passports. As we scrambled to comply I was flooded with the thoughts I had heard about the black market in Eastern Europe and instantly knew our luggage with expensive prescription medicine would be a quality heist for any thief. As I shoved my passport at him, I grabbed the case containing my musical harp, whipped it open, and showed it to the officers. This grabbed their interest and even more their curiosity. With a smile and a quick movement, I struck the 'on' button and began to demonstrate the functions of this unusual looking instrument. I began to play and sing one of the songs the Lord had given me, "*O' the winds of the Spirit are blowing in my soul,*" These ugly overgrown bullies broke into smiles too and became much softer with us. They left the car. The diversion was successful. They never even looked into the big suitcase up on the rack that contained $10,000 worth of goods!

We rather enjoyed the rest of our ride into this new territory, dozing off and on. At one point I squinted out the dark window and *saw something* but I did not know what. I bolted upright and pressed my face against the glass. "Oh, wow, we are in the mountains." I saw the faint glow of dawn beaming over these jagged majestic peaks. I continued to watch as the light of day slowly grew a little brighter. Lila was dozing peacefully. As my awe continued, I saw something that stirred me to the core. I saw a cross on top of one of the peaks. A cross! Then I heard the voice of the Holy Spirit speak to me: "Romania is mine." I closed my eyes, in the wonder of it all. I felt so unworthy to be His messenger.

The entire trip to Romania was chock full of surprises, rescues, and joys. The favor of God surrounded us and I was allowed to speak freely from the pulpits in several churches. I sang the Scriptures and I would quote the verse in *1Cor 1:27 "But God hath chosen the foolish things of the world to confound the wise; and God hath chosen the weak things of the world to confound the things which are mighty."*

Only men were allowed to preach in the Romanian congregations at the time. In fact, the women suffered terribly because they were oppressed not only by living under a cruel dictator, but because of strong cultural practices—their own husbands were oppressive. When Lila and I came to the Romanians, two women without their husbands along, heralding the Good News and displaying freedom and love, they wept. We heard over and over, that we had given them hope for themselves—hope that one day they could recover from the nightmare of cruelty and harshness. They wanted what they saw in us—faith that could move mountains and the freedom to be who they were in Christ.

Shortly after Pastor John helped us settle into our little apartment in Bucharest, Lila and I decided to go for a walk and check out our surroundings. As we walked and smiled, we also received smiles and also some greetings in Romanian. I spoke out one of the lines I had learned: *"We love Romania."* We must have had *'American'* written all over us. When we turned back, we became a little concerned at first, but then worried that we were lost. All of the apartments looked the same! Which one was ours?! We kept walking and praying. As we did, several Romanians came up to us sensing our distress. Of course, we were unable to communicate that we were quite lost. Their concern for us was touching, and they began to follow us like a host of angels. One sweet older woman gave us a big bouquet of red, orange, and white blossoms. When we became desperate, I had the idea to ask one of our angels to use a phone. Along with my gestures and English words one man figured out what I was asking. He led us up several flights of steps and into his apartment. He then gave us access to his telephone. I quickly called and reached Pastor John and told him we were unable to find our way back to our apartment. His reaction startled me: "*What? You are in a man's apartment?! Don't you know you could be raped, robbed, or even killed? Go back to the street and don't let anyone follow you. I will find you.*" Hmmm, I had wondered about all the heavy bars on the windows in this city. I supposed crime was an issue here.

It wasn't easy to shake our small crowd of followers but we managed to politely move away from them. Pastor John did find us and escorted us back to our place of lodging. I learned a lesson I will never forget: when you strike out from your apartment in a strange city, always look back, and memorize your pathway. I am glad we were safe. But I also discovered valuable insight about the Romanian people who cared about us strangers. They are a caring and passionate people.

There were many moments in Romania that opened my eyes and touched my heart in a way that would change me. One such occasion was our visit to an orphanage in Bucharest. Bucharest was dark and dingy. Even the air seemed to hang with dirt and depression. The people walked down the street with slumped shoulders, and if you looked closer, their eyes were red-rimmed and sad. Seeing the many children who were orphaned or abandoned because of the evil governmental controls was shocking and disturbing. I had never before witnessed anything like this.

One of the rooms contained about twenty-five preschool-aged children who were playing. As Lila and I sat down at their child-size table with child-size chairs, the workers began to gather the children and sit them down at the table. Seated next to me was a little girl about three years old who sat in a catatonic stupor. She did not look at anyone and her eyes were blank. There was no affection, no emotion. It was as though the light in her soul had gone completely out. I began to sing a song with my harp. It was the perfect instrument to travel with because of its small size, it ran on batteries and was a suitable sound to accompany the many songs I had written. I sang in English but the soothing Spirit of the Lord went out into the room in that universal language of love. I sang about Abba Father, who takes us into His arms. The presence of love was unmistakable. Literally, I felt like I was Jesus—feeling His love so strong, knowing it was flowing into every heart and soul that was present.

The stricken little girl beside me began to move ever so slightly. I began to watch as she was transformed right in front of my eyes. As I sang, the palpable love of God began to rekindle her soul. Her eyes became alive and she was looking and seeing again. God was giving her courage to come out of her inner prison. She let me hold her on my lap as she soaked in the love which was coming out of every pore of my being and flowing into her. I wanted to sob but kept it in.

The next room had a row of about twelve highchairs with a baby of approximately nine months old in each. As we entered, I had to fight the massive feelings of despair that filled my chest for these innocent children. My inner crying was protesting to the Lord, *"Lord! You are touching the children through us, but what about when we leave? They will remain in this dismal place without hope and without a future! What good is it to be here? Are we really making a difference by coming here?"*

Quickly, I prepared my instrument and began to sing my songs. As I looked up at these little darlings, I saw them looking at me with rapt attention. Their fussing and shrieks quieted and once again, this amazing God poured comfort into their spirits. This was when He spoke to me that, yes, our coming would make a lasting difference because He was healing their shattered hearts and they would have hope and love once again. Later, I gave way to all the sorrow and grief I was storing up inside me as I observed the pain and trauma of the little children. I wept for them but also with great thanksgiving that God had chosen me to come and love a people who were ready for His love—the Romanians.

All of my worries about turning forty and having missed out on life seemed kind of silly now. They had disappeared in a whirlwind of adventure as I had said "yes" to my Shepherd King. I was aware that I was changing. I was being transformed by a force of goodness much greater than myself.

Returning to Spooner, Wisconsin from our mission trip, I sunk into depression. It seemed strange after so much elation to be down in this pit. It had been quite a while since I had been depressed. It was difficult to understand and difficult to endure. Old fears surfaced. A month had gone by. I became frightened that I was losing the valuable ground I had gained in my restoration these past few years. One day, as I lay on my sofa, quietly praying for God's help, I saw a vision. I saw a violent windstorm blowing the branches of trees almost horizontal. In this scene, I was holding onto a slender sapling tree. I was being blown so powerfully that I was literally sideways, flying in the wind, gripping the trunk of the tree with all of my might with arms extended. As I lay there pondering this interesting sight, I heard the still small voice of the Comforter, *"Through your obedience, I have brought about an increase of my kingdom in Romania. The devil is furious, but don't worry, the storm will soon pass."* I began to relax, and sure enough before the week was out, I began to feel more positive. The vision of the storm and me in it, and His words to me, helped me to trust Him through it. I felt joy surging to the top along with a feeling of satisfaction that I had never before experienced. After all of the years of God pouring into me, it was nice to know that his investment had good returns.

CHAPTER 16

Destiny is Calling

Early in the summer of 1997, Carl and I had just completed the celebration of Sean's graduation from high school. We had a grand gathering of family and friends to cheer him as he made plans for his future. It was at this time that we received an invitation to hear a special speaker in a city that was 70 miles away. Carl and I both had an inner urging to attend this meeting and so we did.

The guest speaker was a man who had a gift of prophecy. He was filled with the Holy Spirit and was able to encourage God's people with words that were straight from the Lord's heart. These prophetic utterances were very personal and always encouraging to the person's faith. We are taught in the Bible to exercise discernment and wisdom when someone is moving in these spiritual gifts. It was clear to see that at this meeting people were moved deeply by these messages. When the man came to me, he told me what he saw in the spirit. He saw journals, and many writings that would play a role in the days to come. He said more but it is the reference to the journals that I remember so clearly. I was in the habit of writing down my struggles, frustrations, the outcomes, and solutions. I would write about my special times of hearing the voice of the Holy Spirit. I would revisit these times by reading my journals during other times of discouragement. I have stacks of such journals that are dear to my heart. He also said that by my light many would be led out of the valley. Even more vivid, were the words spoken to my husband. The prophet spoke a word from the Greek language, *"martoos"* which means martyr. He said to Carl, *"I call you Martoos. You are a man who steps aside so others can be helped. You help others and will neglect your own needs and desires because of the love God has put in you. In the days to come you will lay aside your life and many will be saved because of this."*

With tears, I affirmed these words of the prophet. Through my often turbulent days of restoration, my husband stood by me. My deep insecurities would flare and blame him for things he had no control over. The emotional battles I had to fight often flowed over into drama in our home. Many men would have given up and said, "I have had enough." He did say that once and left—I couldn't really blame him. Carl put his needs on hold many times. He returned, however, in a few days, because somehow, deep down, he knew there was good in me and that I was a work in progress. He hoped beyond all appearances that Jesus would bring lasting freedom and change. Jesus did. Little did we know then, but Carl would be called to stand in the spirit to protect me and the work God would do through my hands.

This entire evening was overflowing with expectation and the Holy Spirit's presence. I should not have been surprised that there was more to come. As we left the meeting that early summer night, we were approached by a person who we knew, but not well. We were told about a gathering in just a few days in the Twin Cities. The gathering was a unique event that brought together believing Jews and non-Jews to celebrate a Feast of the Lord called Shavuot. "This is interesting," I thought to myself. As I did, I had a definite reaction—something like electrical impulses flooded my being, accompanied by a resolute decision to attend this mysterious event.

CHAPTER 17

I've Come Home

Several days later when the day came to attend the Shavuot event at the St. Paul Civic Center, Carl was too busy and could not accompany me. My sister Mary, however, expressed interest when I told her about the gathering. So we went together.

My curiosity and naivety about this event was soon replaced with awe and wonder. We sat down in the massive event center that was teeming with people finding their seats. I was inquisitive about the people around me. I observed men with kippahs, obviously Jewish with their prayer shawls draped about their shoulders. Other than my sister, I knew no one. Shortly thereafter, a gentleman who looked very Jewish with a dark beard and kippah on his head, introduced himself and the event. He described the first Shavuot Feast which was the giving of the Ten Commandments by Moses. He revealed that the feast the Christians know as Pentecost was a fulfillment of the Shavuot Feast of Moses and the Ten Commandments. He explained that when the Holy Spirit came in tongues of fire to fill the apostles and those gathered in the upper room, he wrote the law upon their hearts as it is written in the New Covenant. This New Covenant was also written by the prophet Jeremiah. Those who believed in the Son of God, Son of Man, Yeshua, Jesus the Christ, as the anointed one, the Savior would receive the Holy Spirit. Our Master of Ceremonies, Rabbi Ed, a Messianic Jewish rabbi, taught us about what is contained in the Book of Ephesians written by another Jew who came to know the Messiah in a very personal way. Rabbi Ed spoke about the wall of hostility that had divided Jews and Gentiles for thousands of years. He showed how Yeshua, or Jesus in English, brought together all people who believe into one new created being of which we all, Jews and non-Jews, are a part. Rabbi invited all present to enter into worship of our Messiah King together as ONE NEW MAN (mankind). I was amazed to see this written in the New Testament. I had read this particular book many times but never understood the complete meaning or ramifications of this truth. I was astounded. I felt like my eyes were opening to eternal truths that I had been blinded to. As I stood in wonderment and began to lift my heart in worship to my King, the bright lights dimmed and the strains of a hauntingly beautiful song in the Hebrew language began to play: *Baruch Haba Bashem Adonai, Hallelujah*. The notes of the song were in a minor key, and oddly ethereal. I was suddenly aware of the dancers coming up the aisles from behind us. When I looked to see, a breath caught in my throat. A glow and a heavenly warmth came upon me as I gazed on the men and women dancing into the big room, in Hebraic fashion, hands linked together in front and behind, perfect timing, in what seemed like slow motion. I had never witnessed anything so beautiful and I couldn't take my eyes off of the dancers gracefully, gently flowing by. I felt like I was being transported to another world yet it felt like home. I kept hearing those words inside somewhere: *"I am home, I am home, I am home."*

In a flood of unfamiliar emotions, I began to weep, not knowing why. As I released myself to this, my tears turned into silent sobs. My chest was heaving in shudders of weeping. Although I did not know what exactly was happening to me, I experienced a presence of God more powerful than even my encounter with Him in the woods of Wisconsin. I felt an overwhelming sense of love and relief at the same time—a heavenly meltdown. It was as though every burden, every sorrow, worry and weight was being washed away in torrents of a holy river. I felt like I was being baptized into something more wonderful than words could describe. I became aware of a surging love that surpassed all other emotions or sensations. I suddenly realized I was experiencing Jesus' own passionate love for His One New Creation, all of us, Jews and former Gentiles, together in His heart, the very ones He willingly suffered and died a tortuous death to save from the darkness of this world. I could barely contain it. I thought my heart would burst wide open. Then a vision engulfed me. I saw a city, the New Jerusalem. I saw myriads of God's children, each one overflowing with happiness, and each had his and her special place in a massive banqueting hall that was exquisitely adorned in golden light. I saw long tables with expensive settings, chandeliers of gold and diamonds, endless smiles and mirth of the people seated. Some were standing. It was as though it was the wealthiest of all palaces for the most powerful and majestic King of all. I knew immediately that I, too, had a place that was prepared just for me. Because of the deep root of rejection and depression that had plagued my life, the surges of acceptance, healing and more love than I could ever express were a welcome experience. Later, when reflecting on this momentous occasion, I asked the Lord, "How could I even describe this heavenly vision to anyone?" Within the span of a heartbeat, the Scripture verse I Kings Chapter 10 came into my mind. Immediately I grabbed my Bible to find it. It is the story of the Queen of Sheba who had heard of the fame and wisdom of King Solomon and set out to discover for herself if the rumors were true. By the time this noble lady had seen the kingdom of Solomon with all of its wealth and happy, devoted subjects, there was no breath left in her. She not only found the rumors to be true but 'the half had not been told her.' Yes, this described my own experience in the heavenly banquet room very well.

This single event changed my life forever. There was more clarity in my spiritual vision now. I saw more clearly who Yeshua is as the Messiah sent to do what no one else could do. He came to redeem us from sin and death and make us to be like Him and to share in His glorious riches. The realization struck me in greater measure about who I am as His child. The sense of uncontestable acceptance by the Creator Himself resulted in a new level of healing for me. Accepting myself was now something within my reach. I realized that I am loved individually while fitting into this time honored plan of the ages. It dawned on me who the Jewish people are, their calling by God, and the reality of my unity with them. I understood now that their rejection of Jesus as their Messiah had to do with a mystery planned from the beginning of time. A new awareness engulfed me that there exists a master plan to bring salvation to the entire world and all people who would believe—all people who want the light more than darkness.

A new level of faith entered the core of my being, and a profound love for Jewish people came inside of me. It seemed that my Heavenly Father, along with His son, had given me a piece of His own heart of passionate love for His first covenant, people who had suffered for many generations at the hands of a God-hating world. It would be more than ten years later that I would understand the significance of this experience and why God poured a little of Himself into my soul that night.

CHAPTER 18

Restoring What Had Been Lost

At the time of the gathering in St. Paul, Carl and I were both attending the University of Wisconsin. During our hippie days, education was swallowed up in hazy pot parties and a reckless, careless attitude about the future. Neither of us had gotten very far with post-secondary education. I was the first one to have a desire to get a college education. I knew I was smart, maybe even above average. As my children continued to grow and become increasingly independent I had more disposable time in my days. I dared to dream of going to college but had not thought it was something I could actually do.

I began to explore the possibilities. The two-year college nearby was great for starters. I took several courses and my intellect began to awaken and soar to new levels along with my soul. Two years later, I made the decision to go full time to a branch of our state university that was a 90-minute drive from our home.

This was a considerable challenge for me. Although I had healed and been overcoming the past, I had times of anxiety that plagued me. This would occur when I was getting too busy and did not take enough time for myself. Perhaps I was compensating for what I felt was lost time in my life, but I would burn out on a regular basis. Taking care of my family was always on the top of the list, but I had many opportunities to reach out to people who needed help. I did not shy away from giving to others who needed prayer or encouragement. What I had received from the Lord caused me to have a lot of compassion for others. What had been done for me was so crucial to my restoration and recovery. I wanted to give that same level of support. I came to realize and appreciate the energy required to make a difference in a shattered life of a person that desperately needed healing and people to care about them.

A University campus was a radically different scenario for me. Did I really have what it takes to do this? It was comforting to know that this particular student body consisted of 40% nontraditional students. People of my age were all over the campus and in every class.

Immediately after my first semester, Carl and I were in a serious car accident only three miles from our home on our way to pick up an older model truck Carl had purchased. A man, who mistook a rural intersection for a four-way stop, pulled out in front of me as I was traveling 60 miles an hour. The violent, screeching impact spun our car off the road. My head hit the frame hard but I did not lose consciousness. As the car stopped and silence took over, I wondered if my husband was alive. *"Carl!"* I looked and saw blood all over his head. At first he didn't answer me. I called his name again as he moaned and said he was OK. The ambulance took us both to the ER. I had a fierce headache and considerable soft tissue damage that would give me problems for a long time. Carl on the other hand had crumpled the dash board with his shoulder and his head had smashed the windshield. He had several layers of stitches plus a major shoulder injury that ended his career in the forest industry as a logger and heavy equipment operator.

Carl had serious rehabilitation that included insurance coverage for a return to education. Ironically this turn of events changed our entire lives for the good. The long lost hope of college education was now in both of our laps. Truly the Lord Himself was the wind beneath our wings as we embarked on this new world of learning. In three years, Carl was a licensed social worker, and I earned an art degree along with very useful course work and training in transformative mediation. We both graduated with honors and were amazed by the grace of God.

It was during my second year at the University that I had attended the Shavuot feast in St.Paul, Minnesota and was immersed into the truth of the unity of Jew and Gentile believers. I was eager to capture my new found revelation about the Jewish people on canvas. My fervor drove me to my easel in my fine arts building on the University campus. I contacted one of the Jewish believers I had just met and asked him to do a photo shoot for a painting. He agreed without hesitation.

A new vision caused me to attack the canvas with vigor and passion. Creating a palette of blues and browns, both deep and light, I painted with zeal. The emerging image was that of a Jewish man with a prayer shawl and a kippah on his head blowing a shofar, a ram's horn, with the mountains of Israel in the back ground. As I was nearing the completion of this original work, I stepped back from the canvas to get a better look. I gasped! "O Lord!" I breathed, "I see you!" I literally saw and felt the wonder of God's Spirit on this painting. Right there in the middle of the Holden Fine Arts building, on this secular university campus, in the midst of every imaginable art style and ungodly subject matter being produced by other students, my painting was glowing with light. The picture resonated in a way that transcended my world. It connected with eternity somehow. I had no idea at that time, but this painting would make its way around the world and would launch me like a rocket, into my ultimate destiny.

The year after college graduation, Carl and I bought a business. It was a custom framing business. Neither of us had any experience with picture framing. We had no skills but we had the distinct impression that this was something we needed to try our hand at. Starting an art gallery in Spooner had been a dream of mine and it is a natural extension of a picture framing business. Completing our college education gave us a new level of confidence. When we heard of a local framer who was going out of business, we decided to purchase the equipment and give this venture our best effort.

Everything began to fall into place, including an experienced framer who approached us for a job. This woman became our tutor in all the skills and knowledge we needed to run a custom framing business. Carl and I discovered we had an ability to work well together. We worked long hours and "wowed" the community with our beautiful and unique framing styles. We also showcased local and regional artists in the gallery within our shop.

Serving my community in a capacity that required a lot of creativity as well as my artistic abilities was a joy to me. Carl cranked out frame after frame, with great precision. We worked long hours and at some point, I knew I was overdoing it. The effects of too much stress gave me symptoms that were alarming. The new business took a toll on Carl as well. Our time in retail would be short lived, yet it served as a valuable teaching time for both of us. We continued to conquer the mountains of difficulty that our past had set the stage for. Jesus was in charge and His leadership of our lives proved perfect time after time. We grew personally during this time as we learned to work with people and each other as well. We became more outgoing and most importantly, our faith was growing strong.

On another level, our time as business owners was charged with personal drama. My father was diagnosed with ALS, Lou Gehrig's disease. This news was gut-wrenching. Both my parents would need a lot of emotional support and care in the days to come. Shortly after the news about my dad sunk in, our daughter informed us that she was pregnant. She was in her junior year of high school. Either situation by itself was intimidating, but together the impact was overwhelming. We were not in this alone, however. The Lord of love walked with us every step of the way. He never said that we wouldn't have troubles, He said He would overcome them with us—that He has gone before and not to fear.

We loved our granddaughter long before we met her on her birth day. When Holly, our middle child, had become pregnant, we knew two things. This baby was already alive and we would do whatever was necessary to see our daughter through this time. As stark realities of our situation continued to dawn, there was a moment in time that became indelibly etched in my heart. I was with a small group of other believers at a meeting with a guest speaker at the time it occurred. The small but penetrating inner voice interrupted all of my thoughts and anxieties for my daughter; the unmistakable voice of the Lord said, "You must trust me with Holly and the life growing within her!" Strangely, I felt joy stir deep in my being. The angst and fear melted into an assurance of love. This message of love helped me to be loving and supportive to my daughter and carried me through the next year. Our beautiful granddaughter, Serena, was and remains a source of constant love and blessing. I cannot even imagine our lives without her.

The story of my father's illness is tragic in that the nature of ALS is heartbreaking. The progressive paralysis of the body and respiratory system is traumatic. My father was a trooper throughout this experience. After my parents retired and moved north into our neighborhood, we had to deal with a lot of conflict over Catholic doctrine versus my beliefs based on the Bible. It was a stormy season. Emotions flared and tears flowed, but the Lord taught us how to build a bridge of love over these passionate differences. Together we experienced healing and restoration from the conflict. We each had to deal with a lot of personal pain and with forgiveness, giving it and receiving it. A few years later, both parents had become born-again believers when in their sixties. They remained Catholic but they had placed their trust in Jesus alone, not in doctrines or tradition, but a faith firmly built on the Bible. This was evident as we were able to talk more freely about our faith.

CHAPTER 19

Destination Israel

My first trip to Israel was a big event for me. It came during the first Jubilee of Israel in the land—Israel's fiftieth birthday celebration. I decided to take my painting of the shofar blower, titled Jubilee, along. The original oil painting was reproduced as open edition color prints. I thought it just might be an apt gift to give away while I was in Israel. It seemed the Lord was always giving me new ways to overcome the deep spirit of rejection that had plagued my life since childhood. The Bible teaches that it is more blessed to give than to receive. I can vouch that this is true. I gave my artwork out all over Israel and as I did, I spoke of the work of grace in my life through the Jewish Messiah. The response of the people was one of sensitivity and appreciation. Everywhere I went, I gave the picture. Giving my art away gave me a lot of joy.

Before I planned this first trip to Israel, I heard the Lord speak to me. He said, "I am taking you to visit Israel. I want to show you something." It raised my curiosity exceedingly. I wondered if this revelation could pertain to some end time event, or a passage in the Scripture that would perhaps, bring greater insight to me. I really had no idea what this could be but I waited throughout the trip for this 'something' that the

Lord wanted to show me. When it came, it reduced me to tears of gratitude and utter amazement. He alone knows our true needs and He alone can fill them. As we were driving in our tour bus down the busy streets of Jerusalem, I was watching the many Orthodox Jewish men walking down the street in their varying displays of religious apparel: kippahs, satin overcoats with furry hats, black Panama-like hats, and black suits, long fringes. I found it all so very interesting. I felt like the tiniest of ants and was somewhat in awe of the people who, while most did not know my Messiah, possessed a deep reverence for God and His Holy Word. The Orthodox Jews lived their entire lives based on the revealed Word they had. Suddenly a wave of His holy presence invaded my tranquility and I heard this: *"Yet not one of these could ever take your place in my heart."* I was thunderstruck! "I have a place in your heart that is for no one but me? Even the chosen people of the Bible could not have *my* place in your heart?" The thought was beyond all reason, but in poetic fashion, He drove His point home to me. His tender love and acceptance toward me, was taking root deep inside in a manner that could never be shaken again. My first trip to Israel was beyond my hopes and expectations.

My second visit to Israel took place shortly after the 9/11 terror attack on the Twin Towers in New York City. I was to fly out two days after the international flights resumed. It was a travel day like no other. The Minneapolis International Airport was a ghost town. Barely anyone was there. Non-passengers were not even allowed to enter the building. There were a few courageous people who followed through on their reservations. The tension at the airport was so thick, the airline agents were snapping at each other as the effects of terror impacted their nervous systems. The fear was palpable. I, on the other hand, had a knowledge that my God was leading me to go to Israel at this time. I went with confidence despite the cloud of doom that penetrated the atmosphere.

When I fastened my seatbelt and we prepared for take-off in the near empty plane, it seemed as though my consciousness was altered for a few minutes. I prayed constantly inside. I had a strong sense of peace. When we punched through the horrific cloud of trauma that hung over our nation, above the clouds and into the blue, I felt a rush of hope. I was a person of faith in God and that faith made me a person of destiny. I felt strongly that part of my destiny was to be on that aircraft on that day, bringing a breakthrough to our nation from a crippling spirit of terror.

Many Israelis were surprised that Americans would come there at a time when we were facing terror much in the same way the Jewish nation had experienced terror. They were empathic in every sense of the word. I heard their condolences repeatedly even as they themselves were in the beginning of the second intifada. There were suicide bombings taking place all over, especially in Jerusalem.

As I spent time with my American friends who pastored an Arab believers' church in Nazareth, I had the opportunity to sing some of the songs I had written. This took place during the services conducted by my friends there. The people seemed to enjoy my music, because although my songs were in English, the words were directly from the Scriptures. I could give the Bible reference through the translator and the people could follow the song's lyrics in their own Bible. I soon learned that the Arab believers were distraught over the 9/11 terrorist attack. Many of the believers were former Muslims. They were horrified over what had taken place. In addition, some had relatives in the US who were suffering discrimination because of their Middle Eastern appearance.

The songs I sang had special meaning to the Arab believers. I felt as though I was an emissary who was reassuring them that they were loved and in no way being blamed for the terrible terrorism that hit the United States. This began my personal classroom about the diverse groups of people that made up the land of Israel. I learned about people who love and people who hate—people who believed in God and others who believed in a foreign god who was the antithesis of the God I had come to know and love. I would learn about others who were caught in the crossfire of high-powered political polarization. My faith in the core message of the Gospel was unshakeable: Jesus provided redemption for the entire world. His transforming message was desperately needed by all. Tragically, some would prefer the darkness to the light He brings.

My second visit to Israel was full of surprises and adventure. I was in attendance at a worldwide prayer convocation in Jerusalem. People from all over the globe had come to pray for the needs of Israel and the people of Israel, both Arabs and Jews. Part of the plans were to visit a city in the north for which I had a special prayer burden. It was a city high in the mountains of northern Galilee that was known for two things: artists and occultism. I felt obsessed with getting to visit this place. I wanted to pray in an intercessory fashion for the people who lived there. I had a compelling desire that they could come to know the Master Artist who could set them free from the darkness of occult bondage as He had me.

When the day came to embark on the bus for this trip, I was stricken with a terrible headache. The pain in my head was blinding. I did know how I would be able to go suffering from this migraine level of pain, but I found myself boarding the tour bus, anyway. Later I would discover that this head pain was all a part of the spiritual warfare that I was already thrust into. The prayer burden that I had for this city and its people came straight from the heart of Jesus. The ruler of this world, Satan, has an uncanny ability to sense when his dark kingdom is about to be compromised and attempts to thwart God's plan to use frail humanity. It was most likely God's great wisdom that kept me in the dark for a time. Shortly after we began to roll down the highway, our guide announced that we would ***not*** be going to the very city I had joined the tour to visit! She said there had been some security issues. *"What?"* Through my haze of pain and disappointment, I began to silently call to Jesus. This is so wrong, I moaned. I knew I had a divine appointment to pray there. There was no doubt in my mind, and the tour guide's decision to alter course was a terrible mistake as far as I was concerned.

After driving north up the Jordon Valley for about an hour, I heard our tour guide's cell phone ringing. Much to my surprise, she called my name. *"Patricia! Someone is trying to find you!"* she said as she handed me her phone. It was my US friend, Lorraine from Nazareth. "I couldn't get you off of my mind, is everything OK?" I was stunned but replied, "No." As I recounted the situation to her, she asked what I wanted to do. She said she was willing to help me. I jumped at this amazing opportunity. *"Come to Tiberius and pick me up!"* She immediately sensed a God assignment and agreed wholeheartedly. Lorraine was always ready for action. As I waited for the bus to arrive in Tiberias, I took out a sheet of paper from my pack. I wrote a detailed release which stated that I was getting off the bus and would not hold the group liable for my safety. As the bus came to a stop in front of the hotel we were to lodge at for the night, I gave the piece of paper to the driver and the tour guide who were standing together. This situation had never happened before and the driver and the tour guide moved away from me to discuss what to do. Before they could come back to me with their official response, I was gone.

Leaping into the back seat of the car with my friend and her 18-year-old daughter, Laura, I laid down on the seat with a huge sigh of relief. Away we went, driving up, and around the mountain pass, toward the northern Galilee. Oddly, the fierce headache began to lighten noticeably. With each mile, I felt better. I had closed my eyes to rest for a few minutes. It may have been longer but when I opened them again and took in the view, my breath caught in my throat. Amid a dramatic orange and blue sunset, I saw the Sea of Galilee shrinking in the distance as we drove north into the smoky blue mountains. With each breath I felt like I was being liberated from the chains of pain and restraint. Joy began to bubble up on its own. I was soaring to new altitudes on the wings of angels. There was no doubt, the Spirit of the Lord was with us, in fact, leading the way!

Late that evening we went out on the expansive rooftop that had a table and a few chairs on it. As the sky turned inky blue, the entire Hula Valley and the mountains on the other side were visible. In the dusky haze below, the lights popped out, twinkling like the stars. Before me was not only the northern most part of Israel but also Lebanon and Syria. I sat in a chair transfixed by this scene. I couldn't stop gazing. I had no words for this beauty. However, it was not the visual beauty alone that struck me. It was something more. It was a dawning of where I was and why I was there. As I saw in the far distance the road where the terrorists traversed to enter this land of the Bible, I saw for the first time that the violence was not about land, it was about who has the true God. The conflict was about God's true identity. I knew at that moment that all the current events, all the tragedy, the suicide bombers, the constant threat of war, were setting the stage for the greatest revelation that the world has ever known.

We woke to a bright and glorious sunrise over Mount

Hermon. We drank our instant, hot coffee, and chatted as our senses continued to wake up to the new day. Laura had a dream while she slept. When she described the details we all agreed this dream came from the Holy Spirit. We immediately knew that contained within this dream were the details for our prayer assignment. As we prayed together we knew exactly what to do.

First we drove to the nearby army base and parked at the lookout point. There was no one present, although we assumed that electronic eyes were watching every move we made. That did not intimidate us in the least. What we were up to was not a threat to Israel's national security. What seems like utter foolishness to the natural mind is powerful in advancing the unseen kingdom of God. I pulled out my musical instrument, the electronic auto harp which was able to run on batteries. I began to sing the Scripture songs that the Lord had given me during my years of restoration. It was amazing how these songs that gave me life and hope during my darkest hours, were also the very Scriptures that forecast the restoration of Israel and the revelation of the God of Israel. Overlooking the Hula Valley we were now in the opposite direction of the little apartment we lodged in the previous night. In the morning light a gentle gray haze rose from the green and yellow checkered valley floor waltzing about the Mount Hermon peaks. We prayed, we sang and spoke out loud the powerful verses about God's plan for Israel during the last days. All three of us felt the joy of our God as we drove on the high places of Israel, declaring His truth and His glory.

We drove across the Hula Valley and up toward Mount Hermon. We prayed and sang as we drove, getting out of the car at strategic points to agree in prayer. The last stop would be my coveted destination, the city of Safed, which is on a high place.

The city that had captured my heart was now looming in the distance. It was high on a mountain top. It looked surreal to me and I had a queasy feeling hit my gut. I became a little bit afraid because I knew the cruel task masters of darkness that ruled over this city. Having served this dark prince myself, at one time, I could feel the familiar intimidation that stalked my path. The sweet but authoritative voice of the Holy Spirit interrupted my thought flow. *"You have already conquered these spirits in your own life. Do not be afraid. Go to the top of the mountain and dance."* In God's economy, simple acts of obedience can bring light to the dark, and power to the powerless. We drove and then walked up to the park at the top of the elevated city. We sang without instruments and we danced. We danced in worship to the One whom we knew was true. When we stopped, the release of the Holy Spirit was tangible. All of the inner pressure was released into a sense of freedom and joy. We began to laugh. We had been obedient and had completed our assignment. It was at that point that we noticed something unusual laying at our feet. It was the tail of a snake—a real snake's tail. This was almost unbelievable. The victory in the spirit was illustrated in a most dramatic way—a gift of confirmation.

What may seem silly or even childish to some, is the very core of faith to others. When Jesus multiplied the loaves and fish to feed the multitude, this recorded miracle began with an offering from a child. One day we will see clearly how our offering by faith to the Lord that day penetrated the dark atmosphere to prepare the way of the Lord to this city.

My time in Israel ranged the gambit of every possible experience. There were some threatening battles, new revelations, extreme joys, new friends as well as partnering with old friends, all for the purpose of following God's leading for this particular time in history. I was becoming aware of the how different I felt in Israel compared to the more mundane life in the states. My life in Israel focused on spiritual realities that were more powerful than anything I had experienced prior to the calling of the Lord to love Israel. I realized that giving all of my being over to the Lord brought with it the ability to walk in a realm that exceeds the natural.

CHAPTER 20

Transitions

My father passed away in 1999. The man who walked five miles a day, hunted, fished, plowed snow with a tractor, cut trails in the woods so he could ski unimpeded, was reduced to a life consisting of a feeding tube, and an inability to walk, talk or even lift a hand. Though tragic and painful to all who loved him, it was only his outward person that was taken prisoner. His spirit triumphed through the attitude of a champion as he lost his abilities, one by one. The evidence that he had the Holy Spirit dwelling in his being, God's temple, gave him the strength to get through and receive the crown of life. He also had to overcome much in his life of 80 years. Once again the power of the Gospel to empower those who embrace it, made him a different man: a man who feared God more than man and who learned how to forgive. He and I had reconciled our troublous times years ago by now. He was always glad to see me, even though near the end when he was mostly paralyzed, it was only in seeing his eyes light up that I could see his warm welcome.

The day Dad passed on, the home care nurse invited us to leave his room so she could prepare his body. It was my sisters, Sue and Mary, my brother, John and of course, our Mom, who flopped in a heap on the couch. A tangled mess of arms and hugs, we sobbed and sobbed. Our deep pain in watching him suffer day in and day out gave way to pure grief. As we shared in this release, there was an unmistakable whisper of something comforting in the air. It was as though God had His big arms around us all. A month later, we heard a report back from one of the nurses that "When Joe died, the whole house filled up with love." What a nice thing to hear. But, yes, Jesus came to get him and we felt His presence.

This attending nurse whose name was Marge had watched our family in action for several weeks as we came in and out. Dad never wanted to stay in bed like he was some invalid. Carl faithfully came every morning before work to get him out of bed and transport him to the living room sofa for the day. He would return each evening to get him to bed for the night. Nurse Marge asked to be with Dad at various times. Her affection for him was obvious. Hours before Dad died, as we rallied around him knowing the inevitable was at hand, I had a sudden impulse to ask Marge if she had ever asked Jesus into her heart. She said, "No." "Would you like to?" I asked. Right there, as my dad was seeing angels, she said a simple yes and we prayed a simple prayer. I marveled that as one precious saint was entering the heavenly kingdom, another precious soul was entering His kingdom on earth. I felt a wonderful consolation from this. Who knew that just a year later Marge would also leave this earth as a car crash took her life.

When Dad's funeral procession moved from the church to the cemetery, two Harley Davidson friends riding their big loud Harleys escorted the hearse to Dad's grave site. It was a grand parade of family and friends. It was a day filled with sadness and peace.

Six months later, our family sold our home next door to my parent's home, and moved in with my mother. She tried to make it on her own, but the old depression was trying to make new in-roads. She could not sleep in their house since my dad departed. As a result, her mental health began to deteriorate. Our hearts went out to her and we decided to move in with her. We sold our house for under value so we could provide relief sooner than later. Sean was away at college so that left Holly and little Serena, and Shari Ann. Mom was in love with Serena. Our presence really gave her a boost.

Carl and I had passed the torch of the framing shop on to a new owner. In three years' time we actually had begun to make a little profit. But we discovered that retail was not really our 'thing.' It was amazing that we had found a buyer so soon and we were relieved to have a more normal lifestyle.

It took time but Carl eventually found a job in line with his recent college degree. He became a social worker for the neighboring county. This job suited him well and he remained in that position until his retirement. The next year, Carl had to face prostate cancer and underwent a series of tests and treatments. Thankfully, His outcome was favorable, although he endured considerable pain in the process. He recovered quickly, however, and did not miss much work.

I had continued with some course work at the University of Wisconsin that pertained to mediation. Transformative mediation is an interesting form of alternative conflict resolution. Because of my studies and the fact that the concept was quite biblical, I began to believe in the value of it. I became a mediator with the county court systems in our area. Most of the mediation had to do with divorcing parents who needed someone to help them agree on all issues regarding their children. The work was a bit stressful, but the pay was good.

That same year, I become involved with restorative justice, which is a form of mediation involving criminals and their victims. It is a program that brings victims into the justice process to empower them and help them heal. It can also bring about a turning point for those who are guilty of crimes. The program facilitates collaboration with the judge, district attorneys, and other justice professionals to the benefit of all. Through Carl, I received an opportunity to work with the county court judge in the county that employed him and to establish a restorative justice program there. My boss was the circuit court judge. We worked together to give the community a valuable program that would touch many, and give juvenile offenders an opportunity to turn their lives around.

My time as the restorative justice coordinator helped me develop other gifts and abilities. It also helped lift me into a realm of really functioning as a whole individual who had something to offer society. My enthusiasm brought others on board and my administrative and people skills helped create a program that could be sustained by others. I enjoyed this time immensely. The only thing that could have made it better would have been the freedom to speak out freely about the Gospel! My heart ached to tell all! The work of restorative justice had a redemptive quality but it was just short of supplying the real answer. I had to ask myself if this work was what God had in mind for me, or if it was a pit stop along the way to my real destiny.

CHAPTER 21

Collision with Destiny

The stirring for Israel increased with each passing year. I returned to Israel in 2003, 2004, and 2005. Each time I took new art prints to share among the people, both Jews and Arabs. And each trip brought me closer to the people who lived there. I was constantly learning to navigate in this foreign culture. The pressures of the 2005 trip sufficiently broke off any romantic ideas about Israel. It was not an easy place to live as a minority and unable to speak the native language. Carl did not come with me on these trips. He was still in the Monday through Friday work force and was content to kiss me goodbye on the short jaunts. I still had a lot to learn about life in the Middle East but one thing I discovered is that my calling came from above and no matter what kind of frustration I had to deal with, the sure, steady draw to be there did not go away.

Prior to the trip to Israel in January of 2008, I was the victim of a life threatening car accident that took place about 40 miles from my home town in northern Wisconsin. An older man in an ominous looking black automobile, complete with black windows, had abruptly pulled out in front of me while I was zooming south on the highway. In a split second I jerked the wheel and by doing so avoided what would most likely have been the fatality of the offending car's front seat passenger.

The violent impact sent my vehicle careening into a steep snow-filled ditch. I heard myself screaming from instant pain. I thought both of my legs must be broken. An hour later I was being pulled from the wreckage by local firemen and placed in an ambulance. Although I was severely bruised with many contusions, it was a great relief to discover through a CAT scan that I had no broken bones. It took about two weeks just to be able to lay flat in bed without serious pain. The trauma from the accident was a force to be reckoned with. The suddenness and violent nature of the accident imprinted on my sensitive soul. I could barely drive in my little town of 3,000 without significant anxiety and would begin to feel overwhelmed and would cry while simply driving through intersections. The accident took place on my mother's birthday, January 23. My recovery from the accident seemed slow. There were certain physical activities which had been in my routine that I still could not manage. One of them was jogging and using the elliptical for aerobic workouts.

Several weeks after the accident, I was waiting for my doctor to enter the room to give me an exam relative to the car accident. It was always reassuring to hear that the many and varied pains and limitations were part of the normal healing process. It was prudent to know what to expect and what may indicate complications in my convalescence. As the doctor conducted her exam, she was somewhat astounded to find, in my ear, sitting on my ear drum, a tiny shard of glass. She promptly removed the intruder as I sat stunned at the grace of God. Accidents, among other life-threatening events seem to beg the nagging question "Why?" Yes, of course, I was thankful it was not worse. Certainly, the fact that no one died in the accident was a positive note. The driver anxiety that plagued me for a time was not welcomed, but I was trusting the Lord to heal me in all areas that suffered from the impact. This glass particle in my ear was not altogether surprising, but to have my doctor discover it before it could do any damage, left me stunned by the mercy of God upon my life. I have contemplated this scene many times since 2008—especially times when perplexing events warred against my faith and trust in God. Pondering again the disclosure of the itsy-bitsy piece of glass on my ear drum, strengthens my heart and helps me shake off the doubts.

In July, friends from Jerusalem, Roy and Mary, came to speak and tell of their new program designed for healing body, mind, and spirit. Because I was still suffering from the car accident, my ears opened wide as I listened to Mary's presentation of this most unusual ministry. The objective of this healing program was to address not only the bruised body, but mind renewal as well as the *most* important component—the spiritual component. When I learned the venue for the program was in Jerusalem, I knew, despite my financial limitations, that this was something I needed. My spirit blasted off like a rocket as I considered the possibility of participating in this program.

My last trip to Jerusalem had been in 2005 and I was lonesome for Israel. Going to Israel was like a wind of the Spirit each time I went. It was full of God, faith and a river of love for people who needed the love and hope that I could give them. Faith and desire connected inside of me and I knew that I would be attending this healing program. I had that unmistakable sense of God's leading, the familiar electric feeling combined with great joy that struck my spirit like a summer lightning bolt.

My seventh visit to Israel was indeed a very special time for me. I traveled alone, which I did not exactly relish. However, with all the traveling I had experienced by this time, I knew very well that God's grace would be enough to get me there safely. But, missing my connecting flight in New York did not make me happy. There had been so much traffic in the sky that my plane arrived late at the gate. Literally running through JFK with all my stuff was not fun either. I arrived at the departure gate as the door to the aircraft was closing. "No!" came the answer, I may not board. I tried to take this delay in stride, no big deal. Apparently my self-rationalizing did not help. Tears spilled down my face, and I sat down in a crumpled heap. 'Why, oh why couldn't I just be okay with these little trials, without having an emotional meltdown?' Giving myself the same mercy that I gave others was not my strong suit. Maybe that was precisely the point of this kind of trouble. Trusting God *more* always seemed to be the gold lining for me when things did not go according to plan.

Sleep came as I endured a night in a New York hotel. I arrived in Jerusalem the following evening and met up with Roy and Mary, who conducted the Spirit, Soul and Body Healing Experience. This proved to be an incredible time of healing and maturing for me. In addition to regaining the ability to exercise, I learned how to live a healthier lifestyle in general. A part of the program was learning new cooking methods using healthy ingredients such as olive oil, whole vegetables and including healthy protein sources. Mary made it look so easy. I was eager to implement these improvements in my meal planning.

Roy is a singer/songwriter with a mellow tenor voice. He is an accomplished pianist as well. He would sit down at the grand piano in their large open and bright living area and begin to play beautiful praise and worship songs. I would often feel transported into the heavens as I sang along and gazed out the big windows at the desert majesty of the Judean Mountains. Healing from the throne of God was flowing. I knew I was right where the Lord wanted me.

His love was constantly reaching out to me saying "Trust Me!" Emotionally, I dealt with some long held pains of rejection from childhood events. Spiritually, I learned how to let God go deeper into areas of my heart. I had to face the negative self-talk and learn how to replace it with the truth of God's word and what He says about me. This does not happen overnight. I have found it takes diligence and resolve to think new thoughts. It is so typical to be able to edify others but when it comes to ourselves, we tend to justify those old thought patterns that come with a history of feeling rejected and worthless. Using the Word of God in this battle is very powerful. This is why the Apostle Paul calls the Bible our sword—the only offensive weapon listed in Ephesians Chapter 6 which describes the spiritual battle of every believer.

On one of our many outings, Mary had taken her *mento-rees* to a contemplative prayer room in East Jerusalem. Never before had I experienced this prayer style. The holy hush in the room grabbed my attention and turned it toward God. There was no talking allowed in this room that was designed for quiet prayer. Many life-giving Scriptures graced the walls in artistic fashion. The Scriptures reflected the basics that we all need to be reminded of on a regular basis—like forgiveness. Quietly meditating on the reality of being forgiven brought tears to my eyes and reminded me that I can be totally honest with God. Jesus's atoning sacrifice gives me the right to be real with myself and Him, while still being accepted and loved by Him. This is a reality that I live in every day.

In this time of honesty before the Lord, I poured out my heart about many things. Everyone else who had been in the prayer room had left by now. I sat at the table that was equipped with notebooks to write down thoughts. There were also sketchbooks to draw your prayers to God—how fitting and fulfilling to sketch out my passionate heart of love for God. I was alone and let it all out. My fears and doubts seemed to take occasion to overwhelm me and, despite the faith building atmosphere, sobs of discouragement escaped from my body. My deepest pain came to the top. I continued to feel like I did not fit in to the big picture of God's design. The pain of rejection that had plagued me all of my life now seemed more real than ever despite all of the restoration and healing in my life so far. It had a very deep root and seemed to be the most serious challenge to overcoming my past.

I wept from deep inside for a long time. In fact, by the time the sobs diminished, I had before me a mountain of snotty bunched-up Kleenex that was a foot high. I looked around in vain to find a waste receptacle to place them in. The designers of this prayer room had thought of everything to help a person get in touch with God, *how could they not have thought in advance of the problem that now confronted me?!* Tears are the natural response of meeting with God. I felt cleansed yet the pain lingered in my emotions. These familiar emotions were just a sign of something special that God was doing inside. Although I did not have all the answers to my worries, it was satisfying to have given them all over to God. *I had no way of knowing at the time that His answer was winging its way from the heavens, wrapped up in love, just for me.*

The Spirit, Soul and Body Healing Experience had a lasting effect on me and truly empowered me in a greater measure to continue my overcoming lifestyle. When the program ended, I went to stay with a friend in a different section of the city.

Pnina, an American Israeli Jew, was not quite 20 years my senior. Like so many, her Jewish bloodline was not disclosed to her until later in life. Soon after, she came to Israel and received her citizenship. We had been introduced by a man in the ministry, a mutual friend named Emory. We became instant friends. Pnina is a singer and piano player. Although her health forced her to retire in 2018, her ministry in Israel was to the wounded soldiers and the Russian believers. She produced inspirational music CDs and gave them out at no cost. She would travel to the north to encourage the believers there and also teach Bible studies.

Pnina invited me to participate in recording a few songs on her CD. This was really fun. She utilized a well-known family-owned studio in Jerusalem. I found out it required a lot of patience to make a recording. It was not uncommon to have to stop and record the same song again because of a mistake. Two or three of my original songs were on each of several of her CDs.

This time, however, going to the studio would be a little different. This time I was recording my own CD with original, inspirational songs. I carefully selected which songs would work well together. The sound engineer, Ami, and I worked very hard for the entire week. The result was a CD with fifteen original songs sung by me with a little help from Pnina, doing backup vocals on the song entitled *Winds of the Spirit*, as well as Roy, whose voice became the voice of Jesus on three of the songs.

It was quite stressful to record and it was a lot of work. When all of the songs were mixed professionally by the sound engineer, he had me sit and listen carefully. When I heard the finished recording, I wept. I could hear the voice of the Lord through these songs. I became convinced that God could use the music he gave me to help, heal and encourage others. The tears gave way to a happy dance in my spirit.

Could it be that all the valleys and sorrows of my life were leading me to something good? Was there a destiny planned for me, a plan not according to some astrological forecast, but rather a Divine design by the Creator of the universe, the Creator of...me?

CHAPTER 22

An Invitation from Jerusalem

While I was staying with Pnina, she invited me to accompany her to a believers' meeting in the German Colony of Jerusalem. Every Saturday evening, in a seventh floor apartment, believers of diverse nationalities and backgrounds gathered to sing and hear a message from the Bible. Pnina was the regular piano player for the group and led them in rousing choruses of praise about the amazing grace we had received. Many were Jewish people who had found their Jewish Messiah. Some were from Israel and spoke English with heavy accents. There were French speakers as well. There were even Jews from North Carolina that said, "Shalom, y'all," with such a strong southern accent it was barely recognizable to a northerner like me! I was amazed at the incredible diversity of the believers in Jerusalem. Meeting these interesting people who loved the Lord just underscored to me that what God was doing in the land of Israel could only be divine.

It was my joy and privilege to bring prints of some of my paintings along to be given to the people that were present. It was my hope that believers could utilize my artwork to share their faith, by giving it away and opening doors to life-giving conversation. I had been coming to Israel with my art since 1998. At home in our small town of Spooner,

Wisconsin, I had been painting with oils and acrylics. My subject matter had become images that were based on the Scriptures. I repeatedly encouraged the believers there to take the art and use it for God's kingdom. I insisted that they were free. This took a little convincing but finally they began to accept these gifts.

Among those attending the Saturday night meeting was an Israeli Jewish believer named Meir. He spoke very good English with an accent that seemed to combine a number of influences, including French. He was very interested in my artwork. He commented on the bright colors I had used and exclaimed how much he liked my work. I thanked him and gave him several of the larger prints so he would be able to give them away and use them for opportunities to talk about the Lord.

As the evening began to wrap up, this man, Meir, approached me with these words: "Would you like to come and see where I do my volunteer work? Please, let me show you."

"Maybe," was my reply. "Perhaps when my friend from the states, Dolean, arrives, we will come and see. I may call you to set up a time."

He was evasive in a teasing manner when I tried to find out more about this 'work' he did. After I left, I dismissed the invitation in my mind. I was not all that interested in meeting up with someone, especially a man who I did not know very well. This was not the last of it, however.

My girlfriend, Dolean, arrived in Israel and also stayed at Pnina's home. We were excitedly planning our trip to the north of Israel. I was so happy to have her with me and she was just as eager to be in Israel for her second visit. Dolean's arrival in Jerusalem was a happy event. We both knew that we would go to the north of Israel to pray over this land and the people of the land. We were like-minded prayer warriors which made our prayer ministry fun and exciting.

For the next couple of days, as Dolean rested and recovered from jet lag, the man I had met at the Saturday night meeting, named Meir, began to come to mind repeatedly. Sensing the Holy Spirit nudging me, I began to pray in earnest about going to meet him to see about his mysterious ministry. I asked Dolean if she was willing to come on a little adventure. She did not hesitate and said yes.

Pnina instructed us on how to take the city bus to meet Meir. I remember rehearsing the Hebrew pronunciation of the German Colony. "Ha-Mosha-'vah Ha German-'it," I would say repeatedly until Pnina could understand me. The following day we met Meir in a little ice cream shop on a busy street in Jerusalem's German Colony. No sooner had we met up, when Meir beckoned us to follow him. Quickly, he led us down the street one block to big black iron gates which he opened with a key. Inside the heavy gates was a cemetery! Before I could think too much or object, Meir said, "I want to show you something." He led us down the white stone pathway along the long parcel of land that contained numerous old gravestones. There was a long blackish wall that framed the right side and rear wall of the cemetery. The unsightly wall added to the mood created by semi-sunken headstones. There were many tall trees amongst the stones. They were leaning in odd ways as though bowing to one another. One by one, Meir began to tell us the stories of the people who were buried in the Christian Alliance International Cemetery. Meir told us that he volunteered as a tour guide for the cemetery. He told us that many people come through the gates to hear the stories of these historic figures from all over the world.

We heard eight stories that day and it was only the beginning of the over 200 people whose remains were buried there. The first was that of a man named Derek Prince.

This man is well known as a Christian scholar and teacher and author. His teachings went around the world. He was beloved by those who read his works as well as those who knew him personally. Meir was one of them. He said that Derek had mentored him as he did odd jobs for his household. He lamented that Derek had died but he was certainly giving him life with his firsthand account and the love he expressed for this man. Next Meir told us of the man who had the largest monument of all the grave markers. John Stanley Grauel was a Protestant minister who had been on the ship EXODUS and helped care for the Jewish immigrants coming from the Holocaust. Not only did his service help many on the ship but he became involved in the new State of Israel's war for independence. It is said Reverend Grauel played a major role in helping Israel win the war. He was the first Gentile member of the special operations force, the Haganah.

We moved on to the flowerpot grave markers and found out about women who gave their entire lives to pray and intercede for Israel. By this time Dolean and I had run out of Kleenex. Tears ran down our cheeks as we heard story after story of brave people who gave all or significant parts of their lives to live and love with passion and purpose to the people of Israel.

Another fascinating account was that of a Christian Arab man, Jamil Hashweh. He was born to a merchant in 1903 who was traveling through the region of Beersheba at the time of a major revival. The family came to faith when Jamil, one of ten children, was five years old. Shortly afterward, an eye disease pandemic swept through the area and left Jamil blind. He worked his entire life to give better lives to those who were blind. Jamil was the first to translate the Bible to braille. Jamil became highly educated, was an influential teacher, and spoke three languages. He also helped establish the Arab Organization for the Welfare of the Blind.

Although I did not express it at the time, I thought this place is one of the most profound yet silent witnesses of Christian love that I have seen in the entire Holy Land. I was immediately in awe and aware that this was a special place. It touched me deeply to recognize the atmosphere of peace along with a sense of the Divine. But this was only the beginning of a truly memorable day, one that would change the course of my life.

As we wandered under the cloudless sky and the warmth of the sun's rays, we continued to look at the tomb stones and read the words from the Bible inscribed on most of the markers. The cemetery had a long concrete wall on the right that was about 100 yards long or you could say the length of an NFL football field. The concrete wall also went along the back, following the long narrow perimeter of the cemetery. The opposite side wall was constructed of wire and plants and almost concealed the cemetery next door which belonged to the German Templars. In fact most of the plants were gargantuan aloe vera plants, larger than any I had ever seen. Another interesting feature of the cemetery was the trees. The trees were very tall pines and most of them were bending down but in opposing directions. The trees looked like they were dancing to me. "I like this most unusual place," I mused.

Our guide, Meir, then began to relate to us that he, along with the director of the Alliance Church who had oversight in the cemetery, had a vision to have a mural of the Bible painted on the inner walls. Meir said that many people from all over the world came into this place to visit. Most were tourists, some neighbors, and some bereaved. He continued and said that they wanted to find some way to encourage the people who came through the gates and they decided that a mural of the Bible could do just that. Pictures would be a universal language without words. Portraying images in the Scriptures would be a reminder that there is a God, and that He loves the people He created. Meir's tone then changed from spirited to shaky as he stammered a little and said, *"W-would you like to paint this mural?"* I stood in stunned silence. Meir then said, *"We don't have any money for this. You would have to raise it somehow."* It was my turn to stammer as I looked once again at the very long, grey wall running along the side of the Alliance International Cemetery. The massive implications of such a thought struck me in an instant. "W-well...I have to pray about this."

CHAPTER 23

A Surprise Visit

My trip to Israel in the fall of 2008 had concluded with this extraordinary invitation to paint a mural that would be longer than a football field. Once again, the time in Israel created a revival in my spiritual life. Stepping out in faith, believing that the Lord would lead me every step of the way gave me the kind of inner rewards that brought joy and purpose to my life. The invitation to paint the mural was exciting on one hand, however it also brought a flurry of rapid fire reasons why this would be literally impossible for me to accomplish. When I would venture into pondering this possibility, my head would spin and my pulse race. The questions outnumbered the answers by far.

Two weeks after I had returned to my cozy Wisconsin home, an encounter took place that rocked my world. Carl had just left for work and I was sitting at my kitchen table with my Bible opened and my hot cup of home-ground coffee alongside of it. I was in a prayerful place and was bringing to the Lord this incredible invitation to paint a very large mural in Jerusalem. I was pouring out my heart to God about how difficult this would be. "I don't even know if it is your plan for me to do something like this. Are my art abilities good enough to do something of this magnitude?"

As the worries tumbled out, I became aware of a growing sense of the holy presence of God. His warm glow and gentle Spirit were unmistakable and I began to soak it in. I took a deep breath and let go of all the tension that had just accumulated in my body. I then saw a vision of the Alliance International Cemetery with a mural in brilliant colors covering the inner walls. All the way down the cemetery on the right wall and onto the back wall I saw images full of color, although I could not see details. Bright light was emanating from the mural images down in the corner in the back. I saw a small crowd of people standing and gazing at the wall in the corner. I saw what seemed to be the eyes of the people opening wide. I then heard Jesus speak to me saying, *"I am asking you to paint this mural."* I sat in stunned silence, and then began to weep. I fell in love with Jesus all over as His presence and His love washed over me. His voice contained so much love yet was so powerful. He could have asked me to fly to the moon, and I wouldn't have refused Him. The magnitude and implications of such a calling were overwhelming but hearing His beautiful voice, I somehow now knew I could do it. I could paint a mural in Jerusalem that told the story of His amazing love.

How could I say no? He rescued me from destruction and a destiny with hell. I gave Him my crazy mixed up life of torment and He gave back to me a life worth living. Even when I wanted to quit, feeling like I couldn't go on, He put a song in my mouth, and a paintbrush in my hand and made me go on. He believed in me all along, knowing what it would take. He knew that eventually I would trust Him. "Yes, Yes, Yes!" I cried. In His wisdom and love, Jesus knew that I would need to have this personal visit to know that the invitation to paint the mural was not just someone's fanciful imagination or whim. It was a call and assignment from the Lord Himself. Truly I needed to know, beyond a shadow of any doubt, that this was a call to action from the only One who could make it happen. This special time would become a precious memory, one that would urge me on when fierce opposition would try to stop me in my tracks and everything in me would want to quit.

It would be quite some time before it was disclosed to me that the man who first asked me to paint the mural had been prayerfully searching the world over for several years to find an artist. He had been to the US and to Europe as well for various reasons and while on these trips kept his eyes open for an artist who might 'be the one.' In fact, Meir had met an artist in Europe and invited this artist to paint the mural but the Lord told him "No, not the one." After he had met me two years later, the Lord said, "Yes, she is the one."

CHAPTER 24

Ready, Set, Go!

If there is one Bible verse that describes my transformation from 'needy' to 'being needed,' it is this one: *"He lifts the needy out of the dunghill and sets them with princes, even the princes of His people." Psalm 113:8, 9*

The flower child, me—kind of wild on the inside, at one time a hippie girl with daisies in her hair—had become a new creation. The daisies gave way to a blossoming rose. The fragrance of love was beginning to be attractive to others. Instead of always feeling rejection, a sense of value became rooted inside. An unusual phenomenon occurred. People seemed to like me automatically. I no longer had to fight for acceptance. No longer did I feel the need to overachieve to find recognition. I seemed to have stepped onto a fast escalator going up. It was taking me places I had never been before: places of joy and empowerment made possible only through faith. Brokenness has been the hallmark of my life until I met Jesus. Now, born anew, trusting in this good God of grace I had come to know so personally, my life was beginning to sing.

Although the task to begin the preparations to paint the mural were new to me, I seemed to know what to do. I had painted a few murals in my art past, but nothing that would have prepared me or qualified me to paint something of this magnitude. The first thing that I did was to contact the man who was the overseer of the Alliance International Cemetery. This man was the collaborator with Meir in this inspiration and also had the authority to confirm the validity of the invitation to paint the mural. My trips to Israel had taught me that one does not paint on a wall in Jerusalem without official permission from someone. Every tree in Jerusalem is numbered! The authorities in Israel watch closely over all the properties.

With great delight and excitement I received a prompt response from Roger, the field director of the Alliance Church in Israel. He confirmed what had been relayed by Meir and made the invitation official. He, along with Meir and others in leadership of the Alliance organization, desired to have a mural with bright colors that contained images from the Bible, both the Old and New Testaments. Through our email correspondence, we became acquainted. The artwork I had left with Meir a month earlier had made its way into the hands of Roger. He liked my style, he liked the vivid colors. He expressed an eagerness in his emails that I needed to hear. The information, and the confirmation I needed to proceed, was now in my hands.

My next step was to gather people I felt I could trust and tell them about the proposal. Ten people met with me at Nick's, a local restaurant in Spooner. I poured out my story and my heart about the mural invitation. Before I was finished I saw tears in the eyes of several people. When I stopped speaking, one by one, they expressed not only their wholehearted agreement and excitement, but their desire to be a part of the mural in some way. Some wanted to donate funds to help me go and others wanted to come with me, some wanted to do both! I was speechless as I received this reassuring confirmation that truly the Lord would go out before me in this unique assignment. I sensed a deep inner peace that it was time to get out of the boat like Peter did and walk on the water with Jesus. I was thrilled.

There were so many details to think about to prepare to paint the mural. Before I could put one stroke on the wall, somehow the wall had to be prepared and renovated to be able to take on paint that would last. Part of my preparation was to find the proper type of paint that would not get faded in the hot desert-like sunshine of Israel. Then there was the subject of what exactly the first scene would look like? It had to be about creation, Genesis, the first book in the Bible. Yet, there were many ways one could depict the beginning of the world as we know it. Gathering sufficient funds was another whole issue. Should I go alone? Or take others? All I could do was to pour out all of my concerns in prayer to the Lord.

My friend, Dolean, who had been with me in Israel, was at the time conducting a women's retreat at a conference center not far away. I was invited to be one of the speakers and to tell about my mission to paint a mural in Israel. The retreat was a delightful time. As we came together for a special time away, we were not disappointed. We had a great time and heard inspiring messages along with beautiful voices singing praises to God. When I spoke about the mural invitation in Jerusalem, the women responded with whole-hearted enthusiasm. Again I was surprised and delighted that God was stirring people to see what I was seeing. They seemed to know innately that this was no ordinary painting project. The mural invitation came from the heart of our Father. In fact, one woman volunteered her services to raise funds. My heart was doing cartwheels as I took all of this in and thanked the Lord in my heart. He was showing me the way. People all around me joined in the effort and together we hosted a one-of-a-kind fund raising event that approximately 500 people attended. We invited Hebraic dance teams from the area to join in the program. We had several worship teams in addition to a very special guest speaker and musician who is a world renowned violinist, Maurice Sklar. While the music and dancing were taking place, I was painting a large 8 x 16 foot mural on the ground in front of the stage. My friend Karen, who had so graciously volunteered to direct the fund raising, thought of this idea. It was a super idea as it gave me an opportunity to experiment with what I wanted to paint for the inaugural scene of the Jerusalem mural. Helping me were several people who had volunteered to speed up the process and paint along with me. The event was held in an outdoor pavilion in the heart of lake country in the north woods of Wisconsin.

The unity of spirit among the attendees along with the music of gifted Maurice Sklar, set the stage for a tremendous time and offered a rich worship experience for all. The presence of God was tangible. People were touched. One person told me that as soon as she parked and set her foot on the ground, she began to weep, so strong was His presence. We had many positive reports along with quite a few requests to make this an annual event. It was also fun getting to know Maurice and his wife, Devorah. They poured out their gifts and their love. We laughed a lot too. This was a memorable time for me and a perfect kickoff for the adventure of a lifetime.

The proceeds from the event were a great starting point but not enough to pay for all of the expenses this first trip would require. It was August now and I was stumped. What now? As I continued to pray and wait, I heard the Holy Spirit in His still voice say: "Take what is in your hand, go, and I will bring more." This thrilled me! *He said to GO!* When I told Carl what I had heard, he said, "Then you'd better make your flight reservation." What a husband! What faith! This is what I did and that very day, the Lord fulfilled the rest of His word to me. I heard from a lady who had been at our fund raising event who managed a small foundation. She pledged a donation of $3,000—more cartwheels. My faith was growing fast as I took each step on my road to Jerusalem.

CHAPTER 25

Getting Out of the Boat

As the mural painting got underway, there were many lessons for me to learn. Although I had done a considerable amount of painting over the years, nothing could have prepared me for the magnitude of this project. With the tremendous amount of encouragement from all sides, however, I knew I could do it! I will never forget the first stroke of paint *when brush met wall.*

While I was still at home in Spooner, I had painted what I thought was a pretty good composition of creation that would work well for the first scene. It was similar to the event mural I had painted. It felt good to be prepared in this way. When I arrived with my girlfriend, Bonnie L., we were surprised to see that the wall renovations had changed the shape of the first segment of the wall. For the canvas to change shape is an artist's worst nightmare as this affects the total composition and flow of the picture. The workers who renovated and prepared the substrate, had extended the wall at an angle that went from 8 feet on the right to 12 feet on the left. I was aghast! As was my practice when things went out of control in my life, I cried to the Lord on the inside.

I stood back away from the wall a considerable distance. I had already mixed my primary cyan and anthraquinone, several vivid blue tones of paint. I had a three-inch brush in my hand as I stood there contemplating what to do. With a burst of action, I dipped my brush and made a dash for the wall. I began to wing this brilliant blue paint in sweeping, circular strokes, not even knowing where I was going with it. A shape that resembled a giant breaking wave emerged on the wall. I liked it, "*It works,*" I thought wildly as I continued to paint directly onto the wall. I was ecstatic! The wall, the paint, and I fell in love that day. The long wall was no longer formidable. The wind of God had breathed on us.

The more I painted on the wall the more my confidence grew. I began to make quick decisions on what to paint next. My ability to visualize in minute detail helped me to see where I was going with my brush. I literally saw in my 'mind's eye' what to paint and where. I worked steadily on the opening scene of the mural for three weeks. Bonnie L., also from Wisconsin, helped with the background and also some details. As an amateur artist, she enjoyed giving her part. Bonnie helped me get the mural in motion not only with a paintbrush but with her prayers and love.

When the time came to critically assess the scene, I took a deep breath and stood back to take in the entire scene which was 12 feet high and approximately 20 feet wide. Many times I would step back to see from a greater distance what I had been doing. Painting on a large surface, like this wall, has its unique challenges for an artist. This time I stood back to evaluate if I had captured the essence of the vision—not just mine, but the visionaries who invited me to paint the mural. My mandate was simple, perhaps too simple: "Paint the Bible in bright colors," is what I had been told. Exactly how I portrayed the content of the Bible was my decision. I breathed a huge sigh of relief as I surveyed the large colorful scene of creation. Later that day, the field director, Roger, came in through the gates of the cemetery. My heartbeat accelerated. I felt so vulnerable. It was not easy for me to do my craft in a place like this where I was subject to people's observation. *'Focus!'* I told myself, although my consciousness was consumed with the director's reaction to this initial scene. I kept working. I said nothing to elicit an opinion. Roger came over to the beginning of the mural and stood silently for a few minutes, surveying the depiction of creation before him. I wondered if what I had done so far was even close to what he may have envisioned all those years he had been dreaming about a mural in this place. I did not have to wait too long to find out as he lifted his voice to say, *"It's beautiful!"* I quickly looked at his face to measure his sincerity. He seemed genuinely happy. *Oh what relief!* Roger continued to say he was delighted with the artwork.

Together we all began this undertaking by faith. No one really knew what to expect. I had to admire the courage of the Alliance people. Roger's reaction was fuel for me. The boss liked it and that was what I needed to know. The only opinion that mattered more, was *mine. Did I like it?* Did it reflect the work of an artist who understood color, composition, spatial relationships, dimension, direction, and form? I could always find something I could have done better. I had to resist being critical of my work. I had to learn how to decide when to leave it alone and go on. Right now I was so happy I wanted to leap for joy but I was being very conservative in all I said and did at this point. I did not know the people here very well and they certainly did not know me yet. I didn't want to scare anyone with a happy dance… not just yet.

The first scene of the mural is creation. The mural progresses from right to left because this is the way of visual sequencing in Hebrew, the language of Israel.

Meir and I were fast becoming friends. He was in the cemetery most days as I painted. Meir revealed his sense of humor with his occasional comments as I painted various animals into the creation scene. He fell in love with the baby lamb in the foreground of the scene and would talk about the lamb as his pet. But when the puppy appeared, he feigned disapproval. "Patricia! There were no puppies in the Garden of Eden!" I laughed and said, "How do you know? Were you there?" The baby animals were intentionally placed as a memorial to the children who were buried in the front spaces of the cemetery. Since that time, many children who have come in to visit have seen the animals and come running to get a better glimpse.

The first mural painting session was only six weeks long, but it served a vital purpose. The mural was underway. The obstacles, including the fears and doubts this could really happen, had been conquered. All the legwork, the planning, communications with the hosts and staff, wall preparations, paint and supply purchases set the stage for success.

One of the immediate challenges I faced was the simple act of painting while people watched me. I was extremely self-conscious at first. I was painting this mural because I love my amazing God. I did not think my ability was the best or the finest. No matter what the talent or art form, you can always find artists who are more talented and less talented than you are. Mainly my confidence was derived from my strong conviction that the Lord had asked me to do this and I said, "Yes." The more I painted, the more relaxed I became when our visitors wanted to watch.

Until I became more acquainted with the Alliance field director, I would get nervous when he came into the cemetery. Roger was a leader who knew how to make things happen. The pressure to 'perform' could be felt when he was present. Because of my religious upbringing, it was quite easy for me to slip back into the 'performance mode.' But creative flow and performance are not bedfellows. These two forces may learn to cooperate successfully in the practical world, however they can also collide, resulting in collateral damage. Roger's presence was a double-edged sword. It was always a blessing to see him, as his smile and energy were infectious, yet a self-consciousness that took me back years, haunted me at these times early in the painting. It was difficult to just flow with my painting task. Being faced with old ways of functioning called for one thing: more overcoming!

Sometimes I wonder if we really have a choice in the matter of personal growth. Thankfully the master potter who possesses this lump of clay, took my original surrender very seriously and has continued to make me grow up, despite my occasional objections to the pressures that become His tool. I have learned that all of the growing pains result in a gain of more freedom—freedom to be who I was designed to be. Little did I know at the time, however, the burden of painting an epic size mural of God's love story in Jerusalem would bring a weight that was crushing.

As the mural painting continued and a routine was established, I was pleasantly surprised that our days were so interesting. We had many visitors who came in for various reasons; many just saw an open gate and wandered in. I recall the first visitor who came in, looked around and when his eyes lighted upon the fresh mural scenes, literally leapt and threw his hands into the air, shouting, "Yaffe!" Yaffe is a common Hebrew word that means 'beautiful.' This type of reaction made my spirit soar. It would greatly encourage me that the subject matter, along with my art work, was acceptable and spur me onward.

Our first miracle was a man named Ezra. Before we knew his name, the old man would come through the gates of the cemetery and sit on our short stone wall at the entrance. He always had a sad face. He would not talk to anyone. He would stay for only a short time and then leave. He came several times each week. I clearly remember that it was the end of the very first session back in November of 2009 when I was high on the ladder painting when Meir came running. "Patricia, Patricia, the old man wants to talk to us." When I realized it was this particular man, I felt an urgency to come down from my perch and be available to the Lord. The man whose name was Ezra was an Iraqi Jewish man who had immigrated many years before. He spoke little Hebrew and no English. Meir managed to understand that he was depressed and wanted to die. I ran into the shed and grabbed my small picture of Jesus holding the girl, my testimony picture, and explained with Meir's help that Yeshua wanted to save him and help him. We asked if we could pray with him. What happened next is burned into my memory for all of time. We took hands and began to pray. The invisible light of the Holy Spirit came down like a fountain on all of us. I nearly fell to the ground. We asked Ezra if he wanted to receive the Messiah and he said yes. We took hands and prayed as Ezra was born into the Kingdom of God. The transformation was immediate. I saw Ezra smile for the first time. His eyes were gleaming. Meir and I were beside ourselves with joy. We continued to stand there and feel the Lord's presence, communicating through the universal language of love. From that day forward, Ezra would come in through the gates a couple times each week. He would first wave to me and throw a kiss, then he would throw a kiss up to the heavens, recognizing the Lord in this way. He was always smiling.

My first painting session was a real introduction to life in Israel. I was learning how to navigate my neighborhood and how to live among the Israelis. I had to learn to communicate as one who did not speak the language. In stores, restaurants, etc., I often had to ask for help and found most people to be very willing to help me. I had to learn to get past the scowls and frowning faces of people and realize their hearts were most often soft and tender. The yelling and constant debating was superficial and cultural. My conclusion that Israelis were kind and helpful was proven on my bus ride to my flat on the last day of that first painting session. I was so exhausted that I flopped into my seat on the city bus and promptly fell asleep. When I woke with a start, I quickly realized that I had slept through my stop. I had no idea where we were, so I began to look for a young person who may speak English. "Sleecha Bevakashah," I began. "Excuse me, please," in Hebrew, then in English, I asked for someone to help me. Two women in their 40s promptly expressed a willingness to help me. When I mentioned the place of my lodging, they had a disagreement on the best route to get there. They began to argue and then one of the women said, "Follow me." She got off the bus and led me all the way to my destination, with a smile. This warm gesture was such a comfort to me. I felt the smile of God, saying, "See? I take care of you."

There was another very interesting relationship that developed in the early days of painting the mural. The long concrete wall that I was about to paint the mural on had to be renovated in order to have a workable surface to grip the heavy-body acrylic paint that I would be using. The Alliance Church organization hired an Arab man, Nabeel *(not his real name)* from Bethlehem, to do this job. Nabeel had two other Arab men working with him. They created a substrate consisting of white plaster, sand, and concrete. The blackish wall became a soft beige color and served the purpose I needed. The wall renovation alone cost $14,000. I never asked where that money came from. But thanks to the director, what was needed was accomplished and the painting began. Someone in the Alliance organization perceived a valuable asset could develop and was willing to gamble, or more accurately, was moving in faith. As soon as the wall was dry and primed, it was all mine!

The men came into the cemetery early each morning and began working diligently on the 120-meter-long wall. I was introduced to them and greeted them with a big smile since English was not an option. Their presence created an interesting atmosphere in the cemetery. As the mural scene began to develop I became aware of a growing respect from the workers. Once again I had to learn to paint my best with people going back and forth, talking, and sometimes shouting, which Arab men are well-known for. It is not bad or angry shouting. It is just shouting. As the men expressed an interest in the art, I began to grab Meir, who speaks some Arabic, to translate. I eventually told my story of deliverance from dark powers through the power of the Gospel of Jesus Christ. The head worker, Nabeel, muscular, dark, and handsome, could have succeeded in Hollywood. He had a sweet spirit that made me feel his interest in the art and the Bible was sincere. Meir and I continued to display a positive attitude with the men. We offered them drinks and sometimes food. But the most interesting event took place when Nabeel sat down at the table as we were singing songs of praise to Yeshua. Clearly he was being drawn by the Holy Spirit. He had already told us that he liked Christians and often worked for them. I often asked him about his family and in particular his children. We discovered that his youngest child was ill and the doctors could not seem to help him. This was obviously a deep concern for Nabeel. We asked if we could pray for his son. He said yes and so we did, often, over those weeks.

It was very interesting that when I returned to Jerusalem in the spring of 2010, he reported that his life was falling apart. His wife had left him and his child was doing better but not healed completely. I listened compassionately and attempted to encourage him. I even bought a gift of wooden construction toys so he could spend some quality time with his son. This is not a cultural value held by Muslim families. But I told Nabeel how important his quality time with his son was. He always seemed to listen to what I had to say.

One day Nabeel came into the cemetery and asked to speak with Meir and me. He told us that he wanted to be baptized. We were touched by this and helped provide an Arabic-speaking pastor for Nabeel to speak with. Time passed and I did not see Nabeel for a long time, over a year. When I did see him again, because of the language barrier it was difficult to speak with him in any detail other than to express love and joy at meeting once again. I continue to pray for him and that His salvation is real. It is potentially a life and death decision because of the reaction of the Muslim families who become enraged when they lose someone to the Gospel. Many new believers are persecuted and even murdered for their new faith.

The Alliance Church has a ministry to the Muslims as well as the Arab believing church here in Israel. The first believers of Arab descent that I became acquainted with were Alliance staff. I met Ramaz and then later his wife Mary, and over the years their two children as well. Ramaz is the property manager of the Alliance Center on Prophets Street. Ramaz is a picture of a true servant of God. His diligence and kind spirit reflect the One who saved him. Ramaz has helped me many times when troubles came. Mariam is also on staff, a young Arab woman who has business acumen that has been a blessing to the Alliance administration. I have come to really love the people who live and serve here and appreciate their struggles and pressures. Rachel, also, was on staff for most of the time when I was painting the mural. She has become a good friend. Life there is not simple nor easy.

The first crew of helpers from home came during the fall

of 2009. Dolean brought Sherry, Mary, and Sandy all from Wisconsin. These precious prayer warriors came with a lot of joy and encouragement. They helped get me set up in the mornings and they also helped paint some of the background colors on the expansive wall. The mural consists of many layers of paint and color. They lodged at a monastery nearby that had a guest house. As they adjusted to life in Jerusalem, they also became aware of the difficulties that exist in this wonderful place.

CHAPTER 26

Drowning in People and Paint

Session number two took place in the spring of 2010. During the winter months, our very creative God was busy stirring a new crew of helpers that would come to assist. We were all so enthusiastic back then that the sky was the limit; the more the merrier, right? I was about to discover some of my own limitations. Painting the mural changed me almost as much as the deliverance ministry. It was very humbling to have to face myself and my areas of rigidity. But then did I ever claim to have arrived at a place of spotless perfection?

The first to arrive in Jerusalem in March 2010 was Bonnie L., Bonnie V., and Gene and Lila. All were friends. All had been in Israel before so this was helpful. Gene and Lila already had skills in navigating this Middle Eastern turf as they had spent time in Israel in 2005. I felt a lot of responsibility for those who came to help me. Yes, there were dangers here beyond the scope of our familiar American middle class existence. And yes, it took some time to learn how to be here safely and in a way that would yield a positive experience.

As much as I wanted the help from those who came, the reality of having people around me who needed to have my direction in order to *be* helpful was quite difficult for me. I had to leave my artist mode and pull up other skills like organization, interpersonal skills, and communication skills and on the list goes. I do possess these but feeling a demand from all of them at once was almost debilitating to me. I felt overwhelmed and my joy turned to worry. My demeanor showed it and I began to apologize to my crew for this. This kind of pressure brought out my old nature. I tried to explain that if I looked and sounded less than happy, it was from the pressures I was feeling. I so wanted to convey a message of love and gratitude to my fellows but instead I sounded crisp and even mean at times. I discovered that the only remedy was to apologize. The Holy Spirit pricked my heart when an apology was needed. A deep work took place in me each and every day that I painted the mural. My friends were also stretched beyond their limits at times. Grace takes on new definition when you are the one who needs it from others. We got through our moments. With our collective blood, sweat, and tears, the work of painting the mural lurched forward. I offer my wholehearted thanks to these precious saints who came at their own expense and stood by my side through thick and thin. I applaud you and thank God for each of you. Also to the many you will still read about in the coming pages.

Most of our crew lodged at Roy and Mary's ministry house on the north side of Jerusalem. They have a lovely home with great accommodations. Mary would cook mouth-watering breakfasts for us and Roy would often bless the start of our day with a song at the piano. There was much laughter as Lila would recount story after story which bore retelling. This would spark other people's memories and much entertainment would commence. Though we had to drive through the gnarly mess of Jerusalem traffic to get to the mural, it was worth it for this sweet oasis.

The second half of the crew arrived two weeks later. This

threesome included my husband Carl, his sister Charlotte, and our dear friend, formerly from Spooner but now from Utah, Paula.

It was especially exciting for me to have Carl come. It was his first trip to Israel. Each time I went to Israel I would beg him to come. But he would flatly declare that when it was God's time for him to come, he would. At that time I had not been aware of a promise he made to himself when he was traveling home from his tour of duty in Vietnam. He told himself he would never again leave the United States of America. Carl went into the service as a Marine and emerged a hippie, like so many other GIs. They had experienced a horrific nightmare that lasted a year and couldn't forget it fast enough. Drugs and lots of alcohol were the primary antidotes. When I met Carl he had just survived a car accident that could have taken his life. He was high and drunk when he was introduced to that telephone pole in the middle of the night. That was so long ago. Carl received Jesus two years after I did. His life, too, had experienced a gradual metamorphosis. As in my case, facing his past to be free for the present was a task he could not escape. He had made the decision to come to Israel when his sister said to him, "If you go, I will go." He knew it was time.

Most memorable about Char, Carl's sister, was that once she sized up the daily painting routine at the cemetery, she began to assist in the details without even being asked. She would bring my big water pail out, and other assorted supplies. She also helped paint backgrounds, as did Paula.

Paula's most valuable contribution was playing her clarinet at the praise and worship time that we had each day. Paula is a gifted musician who also plays by the Holy Spirit. The notes of her love offering to Jesus resounded in the German Colony and flowed out beyond the gates into the rhythms of Jerusalem.

One Friday evening, Carl and I went off by ourselves to meet some friends for dinner in Abu Gosh, which is a small city just outside Jerusalem. It was Erev Shabbat, the evening before the Sabbath Day, and traffic had just begun to thin out. I was driving the Alliance's old Nissan van. This was the vehicle I had learned to drive with in Jerusalem. Thankfully it was small for a van, yet quite visible to others who had to avoid me as I learned to navigate the heavy traffic.

We had just entered the long Arazim tunnel on Highway #1 when a motorcycle zoomed up from behind us going about 80 miles per hour. We had just picked up speed as the tunnel was quite void of cars—that is, until we began to round the big right-leaning curve in the tunnel. There was no way to know that just ahead, traffic had backed up and had come to a dead stop. Instinctively I knew the cyclist was in trouble. No sooner had this thought flashed through my mind than we heard a loud crash and saw an explosion of man and cycle ahead. He forcefully hit the car in the right lane, his motorcycle exploded and flew to the left as he was thrown and lay in a heap in front of us. We stopped just in time to avoid running over him and prayed that no one would rear-end us from our screeching halt. Carl and I immediately began to pray. The ambulance and paramedics arrived with uncanny speed. The cars now lined up for a mile back had to squeeze over to the side of the tunnel to let the emergency vehicles through. We saw the young man twitch and knew he was still alive, but it was obvious that his body was a bag of shattered bones. He was not ready to die! This young Jewish Israeli did not know his Messiah yet. I prayed pools of tears for this man. I went out of the van and went closer to him and I prayed—prayed and wept. Though I thought the medics would shoo me away, they seemed encouraged by my presence. However, the moment came and one of the medics said in partial English, *"Please close your eyes, we are going to open him up."* I got back in the van then and kept praying and weeping for this man. The heroics of medicine were not able to save him. He died in front of our eyes. All had to wait for Zaka, the Jewish organization who handled the deceased in Kosher fashion. By the time they took him away, most of the traffic had backed out of the tunnel. We had to do the same. A police man began shouting at me, telling me how to back up. I was already traumatized and agitated so much that I backed up right into his squad car! Then he yelled at me in twice the decibels. Carl intervened and gently guided the tedious back up process between all the emergency vehicles. We were then stopped by a police officer who wanted my statement to record the details of the crash. By the time we returned to the house, I was done for. The trauma of witnessing this untimely death was more than I could bear. I went outside on the balcony that overlooked the Judean hills. That young man is so much like the rest of the Israelis—zooming down life's highway, so determined to live and definitely not ready to die. They do not see what is just around the bend—sudden death—and they do not yet know their Messiah. My tears would not stop as I gazed at the barren landscape from Roy and Mary's balcony. I heard the door open and close and then heard these words: *"It was not an accident that you were the ones at the scene."* It was Roy speaking: "We do not know the reality of the time and space between life and death and heaven and hell. Your prayers and intercession were heard. It was not an accident that you were there." For the first time my sobs subsided and my spirit calmed. These words resonated inside of me as truth. My only resting place was to believe that God heard my prayers. His name was David Levy; he was 26 years old. The next day I went in to the police station in the Clal building on the top of Jaffa Road to inquire about the family of the deceased. Having worked in the field of restorative justice, I knew that for families to talk with the last person to see their loved one alive can bring healing. I wanted to offer my time. When the police realized who I was, the primary witness of the now well-published motorcycle fatality, they almost jumped to get me into an inner office to talk to me. Before I knew it I was sitting in the office of the ranking detective who questioned me in great detail. They said there was controversy that a car in the tunnel scene was responsible for the crash. This was ridiculous and I told the detective why. As I retold the traumatic event, the tears began. But I wasn't the only one whose eyes were wet. The detective became very soft and thanked me for "being with them in this tragedy" and for having helped them. This was a difficult experience for me. I couldn't drive through the tunnel for a long time and when I finally did, I had to pray or sing my way through it. Through this experience, I felt closer to the Israelis than before.

Soon it was time for Carl to return home. He was still gainfully employed as a licensed social worker and had used his vacation to be able to come. I asked not to go to the airport with Carl, Char, and Paula because it would be too difficult to say goodbye there. Here in Jerusalem was better. So once again we grabbed for the grace of God to be apart for a season.

CHAPTER 27

Hitting the Wall

The life of mural painting had many types of ebbs and flows. The number of scenes on the wall began to increase and the mural was growing longer. Some scenes were completed quite quickly and some took much time. But it was not up to me. The mural was a labor of love through prayer and faith. I learned many things as I continuously sought the counsel of my Teacher, the Holy Spirit. I learned how to mix large batches of paint for my helpers, as well as how to use rags instead of brushes to cover large sections of the rough wall. My paints lasted a long time because I preserved them through wraps of plastic so they would not dry out. The only supplier of Golden Heavy Body Acrylic Paints was in Tel Aviv. They sent a courier with each new order of paints.

One lesson that I had to learn via the school of hard knocks is how vital it was to pace myself. I was exuberant and so desperately wanted to feel like I was accomplishing the painting of this epic sized mural. I was much too intense at times. In my zeal, I kept painting right through the Sabbath and that was a big *'no no.'* By the fourth day of the next week I was so exhausted that I could barely lift my brush. My spirits were low and I wanted to quit. I recall standing by my latest work, a gusher of tears erupting, streaming down my face. A new friend had entered the gates and approached me. It was quite clear to her what the problem was. "Patricia, why don't you get in the van and drive up to the Galilee for a break from the city?" Somehow the grace to do just that entered my being. "You are right!" I responded softly. I cleaned up, packed a bag and looked up a telephone number I saw in the Grapevine, an online publication to assist believers in the land. I had seen the number of a bed and breakfast in Tiberias that sounded nice.

Driving in Israel was still novel at that time. It took a certain amount of courage to drive alone up the Jordan Valley to the north, not knowing exactly where my destination was. But once again I was amazed by grace. I got in my van and it was like someone else was doing the driving. I had to fight off a little anxiety, which can play with me when I am on the edge of burnout. When I reached the outer areas of Tiberias, I really did not know where I was going and I had no GPS at that time. I had gotten quite lost in this city in the past and knew it could easily happen again. Just as I started to worry, my eyes suddenly flashed on a sign with the name of the hotel that was right next to the bed and breakfast! *Really?* This would be too good to be true. I made two more turns and there was the hotel and there was the B & B. I entered the house in a surreal mood. The hostess was an artist herself. Artwork was hanging throughout her home. She helped me settle into my room and then invited me to join her and a friend on the big balcony overlooking the shimmering Sea of Galilee at night. As we three sat and gazed at the twinkling ethereal lights of the valley, my hostess and her friend began to sing a worship song to King Yeshua—their God and my God. I was in the company of family. I was so thankful. I collapsed into His arms in sweet relief.

CHAPTER 28

What Next?

The mural progress suffered constant interruptions. I had to learn not to stress out when my progress seemed to be at a crawling pace. If I felt too much pressure, then it was more difficult to discern which interruptions were hindrances and which ones were golden opportunities to talk about the Bible and the Lord. Today's interruption turned into a Divine appointment. Roger came to the cemetery unexpectedly early on Thursday morning with two other men. He asked if I could come off the ladder and talk about the mural to his 'bosses.' The two men were heads over Europe/Asia Alliance operations. One of the men, Jerry, was in orientation training with the other older man, John, who was preparing to move into a different position. John said he had been hearing about the mural and was very excited to see it for himself. Just as I was beginning my presentation giving the men the back story of the mural, a young IDF (Israel Defense Force, which is the name of the Israeli Army) soldier came into the cemetery. He was very shy and asked if he should leave. We invited him to join in the mural 'tour.' Because the young man was obviously Jewish, I presented the way I do to other Jewish people who come in. We had some lively discussion about various mural scenes of the

Tenach as far as the work was finished. John and Jerry had a front row seat to see how the Lord was using the mural to touch people's lives. After the soldier left, we continued to discuss many different aspects of the mural, present and future. John said very officially that he wanted to thank me on behalf of the Alliance worldwide for the ministry of this painting. The concern I had about unwanted interruptions gave way to a thankful heart for this break in my day. Meeting with the three men gave me renewed courage to battle against those times of feeling overwhelmed when I looked down the long blank wall.

Another interruption occurred when I had my fingers near the tall iron gates of the cemetery entrance when they were about to slam closed. I had just opened the gate to let Meir in and was talking to him while attempting to close the gate. Somehow my right thumb got in the mix. The instant excruciating pain told the story. It is similar to having a car door close on a finger, except this door was three times as large and three times as heavy when it landed on my thumb. I tried to push through the misery but the next day the constant pain knocked me out of commission. Ellen, the director's wife offered to take me to the clinic. Normally I avoid doctors and dentists if I can, but this time I was ready for anything that could bring relief. As we drove through a part of Jerusalem that was unfamiliar to me, we stopped in front of an Arab clinic. I checked in and soon was called into an exam room. The Muslim doctor examined my throbbing bluish thumb and promptly grabbed a drill! NO! I wanted to run screaming out of that room. But the doctor was so kind to me and gentle that I did not resist. He began to drill micro sized holes in my thumb nail as I courageously looked anywhere but at what he was doing to me. Suddenly he gave a little shout of victory and blood spurted out in all directions. The gross pain subsided quickly and before I could say, "Thanks a lot!" my hand was wrapped and I was whisked out of the room.

Getting to know Ellen was not easy. She was friendly in a non- committal way. I could feel her shields up. Because she worked full time in the Alliance office and was the director's wife in addition, she worked under much pressure and most likely needed to keep good boundaries. I was undeterred. I made myself a promise to win her trust and become friends.

After resting for a day I went back to my painting assignment. On one particular Friday afternoon a familiar face emerged from the open gates. He was a regular visitor to the cemetery to place fresh flowers on his first wife's grave. He is an Israeli Jew with Russian descent who just happens to be a professor as well. He and his wife have come to be beloved friends over the years. He has a great sense of humor and a classic Jewish face. I couldn't help wondering if he might not permit me to use him as a model for the face of Abraham on the mural. The model for the face of Abraham had to be someone special. After all he is the father of faith for all people. As I have said to many visitors, "Before there was Torah, there was Abraham, a man with child-like trust in the almighty God which was counted as righteousness," the Bible tells us. Additionally all the promises to the chosen people began with Abraham so *he had to look Jewish*!! To me, this man fit the bill. As I spoke with him that day and lightheartedly broached the possibility of a photo shoot, I was delighted to hear that he was open to this idea. He is a humble guy who certainly wouldn't have to be. I love that about him. He is a sought-after lecturer and travels all over the world. Out came my camera and I quickly snapped several shots, mostly close-ups of the professor's rugged countenance.

The painting of the patriarch did not take place for another week. I used the light projector to keep the image in perspective. I had decided that Abraham would be the largest figure on the entire mural. His ability to be a visionary and follow the leading of God Himself is alone admirable but also, He is the progenitor of Israel and the chosen people. He is the father of the miracle baby Isaac, the child of the promise. After all, we are in the land of Abraham, Isaac and Jacob. After I had his outline drawn and the background painting done, I heard a shriek and then heard my name. *"Patricia! No, no, no.* He is too big. *Too big!"* Meir became very upset that I had made Abraham so immense. This was not the first time Meir decided to be an art critic. There were several times he debated some of my decisions of what went on the mural. I always won the battles but occasionally had to fall back on Roger to establish my authority that the ultimate decisions about the mural scenes belonged to me. Meir is outspoken by nature and frequently made his thoughts known, as do most Israelis. But this time was too much! His wild reaction almost intimidated me enough to back down on my decision to make Abraham super-sized. Since that time many visitors who view the mural express how much they like this imposing figure. Eventually, Meir too came around to voicing his approval and told me how much he liked the XL Abraham.

Almost every morning, Meir, as well as some new friends from the neighborhood, would gather to worship the Lord in song and prayer. I would lead the songs with my electronic autoharp, the QChord. As our voices rang out, our love for Yeshua would pour out too. Most times we would sense His sweet presence. He would lift every care and strengthen our confidence that we were in His will. He also renewed our trust in Him. As the melodious sounds floated upward into the atmosphere of the German Colony, we could glimpse into eternity for just a brief time and know that our presence was impacting the earth.

There was an unusual occurrence in November of 2010.

After a tough morning of painting in the midst of spiritual pressures of many kinds, we received a phone call from one of the Alliance staff across town. There had been an attack on the Alliance Center. A fire bomb had been thrown through one of the rear windows downstairs, which set the building on fire. There were ten people sleeping in the dorm rooms who were from an Alliance Church in Olympia, Washington. They had been at the cemetery just a couple days earlier, raking pine needles, weeding, watering plants, and cleaning up the place in general. They were a dedicated, hardworking, but fun group. They have returned to help several times over the years. It was a treat to have them spend time in the cemetery. Now we had a report that two people had to be taken to the hospital nearby.

Rose, Jessie, and Elisheva were some of the believers who had come to the cemetery to sing and worship with us that morning. They accompanied Meir and me over to the Alliance to pray and encourage the people there. When we arrived we went downstairs and beheld the damaged, charred rooms. We were shocked and had to step on items over the flooded floors just to get into the room. Director Roger told us the entire story. We were all thankful that no one died, which could easily have happened. The Lord was faithful in His protection from serious harm. The Alliance is located right next to the most religious section in the entire city. The ultra-religious have a lot of control in this city and often demonstrate against those who do not hold to the laws of Judaism. Some immediately began to suspect this was an action from that sector rather than an act of terror of a Muslim jihadist.

It left me with a strange feeling as we surveyed the charred rooms and broken window. This deliberate violence perpetrated against a Christian church was a vivid reminder that serving the Lord comes with a price tag. A price we must all pay on occasion—but what an honor to suffer for the Gospel.

There was an existing insurance policy, thankfully. The Alliance had a lot of hoops to jump through, including police interviews and investigations by insurance adjusters. This all took a lot of time and money that was not in the planned budget, but eventually the Alliance underwent serious renovations and repairs. The outcome was a new and beautiful guesthouse dubbed The Hermitage. Rugged Jerusalem stone-work graced the inner walls as well as a new community kitchen with wooden cupboards and appliances. The guest rooms were also new now and very inviting.

Later that evening I drove the 35-minute drive to the small city that will remain unnamed to protect the small congregation that was my destination. After a day filled with a conglomeration of worship, distress, fear, tears and trust, to be in the presence of familiar faces and longtime friends was like being wrapped in a soft, cuddly comforter. Gary and Lorraine were my pastors and friends in the 90s in my home of Spooner, Wisconsin. They did not spend much time in the states because of their calling to serve in Israel and the Middle East. But during the time they did spend there, I had the joy of getting to know them well and becoming close friends with them and their two children, Laura and David. Our two daughters were the same age and became friends through the church.

Lorraine is a gift. She is a woman who is passionate about the Good News and making disciples of all tongues and tribes. Throughout their time in northwestern Wisconsin, she maintained her zeal for the people of the Middle East. She loves the Arabs, both Christian and Muslim. Yet, she reveres the roots of our faith and the Jewish people who brought us the Bible as well. She is very loving and demonstrates that love through action whenever she can.

Gary is a prophetic preacher and teacher, as well as an intercessor who endured many battles through fasting and prayer to gain breakthroughs for the Gospel both here and there. I have always said that Gary is God's secret weapon and will aim and launch him in amazing ways, especially just before the Lord returns. That evening in their home congregation, Gary preached on Zechariah 12 and it was powerful. We are living in 'that day' and God is preparing us all for that which he will orchestrate with Jerusalem as was foretold by the prophets.

When I first began to visit Israel, Lorraine was my teacher regarding how to navigate the many features of this land which was so very foreign to me. We would take off in her van and drive all over as she accomplished her daily 'to do' list. We would have a steady stream of lively conversation sprinkled with valuable information as I, her student, readily soaked it all in.

This night I fell into the fellowship of the Body of our Shepherd, Jesus. I cherished the warm presence of the Holy Spirit. The gentle breeze blew away the cares and concerns of the day. I felt safe and I was.

CHAPTER 29

Springtime in Jerusalem

Painting the scene of Moses was a fun challenge. Many artists have portrayed the hallmark event of the Hebrew people. I refused to look at these other artworks for two reasons. I desired a visual interpretation that was fresh and nontraditional and I did not want to inadvertently be influenced by another artist's work. It became clear once again, that I was the understudy and the Lord was the artist. Sometimes He would put a full color picture in my mind and I would paint it. At other times, I would just start with the colors I wanted and start swirling my brush on the surface. I would see some interesting patterns and effects that just happened and then more ideas would come the more I painted. The painting of Moses was a combination of these.

The large 12-foot wall I had been painting on since the beginning was now sculpted by a Jerusalem stone wall that elevated the mural wall up into the air by approximately six feet. The mural wall now loomed to a height of 15 feet as it sat on the picturesque old wall. The scene of Moses parting the Red Sea fell right into the nook of the two different sizes. It made a perfect place to put a large scene of the giant waves displaying the parting waters with Pharoah's chariots in pursuit that then narrowed to the safety of the other side and jubilant celebrants like Mariam with her tambourine.

Preparing the background was routine but the job of painting the clouds over the Red Sea beckoned to my spirit of adventure. In order to have bright lights in a scene, an artist must employ a painting technique called chiaroscuro, developed during the time of the Renaissance. It contrasts light with very dark colors to maximize effect in two dimensional compositions.

As I began to paint the dark sky over the Red Sea I noticed something high on the mural that I didn't paint. I got off the ladder and looked again. There seemed to be a light on part of the sky. I said, "Wow Lord, I like that!" I thought it was from the sun but it was impossible since the sun was down behind the mural wall. I sat on the nearby bench. This did not make any sense to me. Where was this light coming from? It illuminated the exact place I had been contemplating to paint the heavens opening in advent of this miraculous parting of the Red Sea. Then these distinct words came into my mind, *"You had better paint it before it disappears."* By the time I mixed the paint and went up the ladder the light was gone. So I painted what I had seen. I was thrilled that the Lord encouraged me with a supernatural sign..

CHAPTER 30

Learning the Hard Way

During this mural painting session, I had decided to rent a tiny flat that my friend Rose had rented. Rose was a volunteer who worked for the Christ Church in the Jaffa Gate of the Old City. It was her time to leave the country for a year as required by Israeli law for those with a volunteer visa. Rose had an additional ministry of prayer walking. Although I met her through a friend, I became acquainted with her when she would stop by the cemetery and ask if she could pray. I would always say, "Yes! Please pray!" Rose eventually came to join in our worship times. She was the quiet sort but devoted to the Lord and faithful to her calling to be in Israel. She became a valued prayer warrior and support to me in the developing ministry within the gates of the Alliance International Cemetery.

Her tiny flat was so small I couldn't imagine living life there for three months. Rose had done it for several years. The price was right and so I decided to do it. The biblical holiday of Passover, or Pesach in Hebrew, was fast approaching and I decided to get a new mattress. It was not difficult to find a suitable mattress since Talpiot, the shopping capital of Jerusalem, was only blocks away. The mattress fit in the Alliance's Nissan van I drove. However, when I arrived at the apartment, which was a flight of steps up from the ground floor, I did not know how I would manage to get the mattress up those steps. As I was contemplating this task, a thought whispered, "Ask that young woman in the next flat to give you a hand." In retrospect, I am quite sure that was the voice of the Holy Spirit delivering some reason to me. Reaching back to the independent ways of my old days when I could be 'Amazon woman,' I reasoned back: "I can do this!" I hoisted the mattress on my head and slowly made the ascent to my flat. I heaved the heavy object inside and felt like I had accomplished something amazing.

Carrying the single size mattress up to my little home away from home was a feat that I should have reconsidered undertaking. The next day as I was sitting on my tall stool at the tiny window counter reading the Post, I made a move to grab my coffee mug and without warning, hot searing pain racked my entire lower spine. I literally could not move a muscle. This had never happened to me before. I have heard of others who had their back 'go out,' but I never understood what they meant by those words. Clearly, my back went out of commission in the space of a solitary heartbeat. I tried to get off the stool, but that proved almost impossible. With excruciating effort I lowered myself off and tried to walk. No, walking was impossible. The pain was off the 1-10 chart! I called Roger on my cell. He is the person who I reserved for serious issues and big trouble. I winced as I related what had happened to me. He told me about Ellen's chiropractor who had helped her considerably and offered to take me there.

Reluctantly, I conceded and had to allow Roger to help me in and out of the car and all the way into the office of this Jewish chiropractor. The chiropractor was an older gentleman who had made Aliyah from the United States. I had to visit him often in the next few weeks. I had X-rays taken at a local clinic so he could know better how to help me. The films showed that when I carried the mattress up, the weight of it crushed down on my disc, which was already thin. When I would ask if he thought I was showing signs of improvement, he would say, "Well, you are not screaming as loudly as you did at first." I don't think I actually screamed by my definition of screaming, but I guess the pain did produce plenty of groans as he worked on my spine.

I had to take some time off from painting the mural to heal. But even as I felt I could be on my feet for a period of time each day, climbing the ladder did not do my back any favors. Now I had a problem. I became discouraged and thought it might be best to fly home to recover.

One day when I went to my chiropractic session I couldn't hide my depressed affect. "What's the matter?" his voice boomed. "Sit down here and talk to me." Oh no, I felt so vulnerable and withdrawn. How could I be honest with the guy? I simply told him I was discouraged because it was taking so long for me to heal. The artwork of the man blowing the shofar that I had given him on an earlier appointment was hanging proudly on his wall. He then told me his own story of being in a motorcycle accident that crippled his leg. He told me personal details about his struggle to go on with life with a handicap. "You must not give up! Never give up! Be happy now, be courageous!" The fact that he cared enough to treat me like a daughter helped me climb out of that pit. I felt the tenderness of my Daddy God in that man.

I met with Roger and Ellen at the Aroma restaurant down the block from the cemetery. We talked about this situation I found myself in. Roger had an idea. He knew of a man who attended the Old City congregation who was out of work for a time and wondered if this man could help with and apply some paint for me, especially on the tall areas of the wall. I liked the idea.

Later in the week, an Arab believer, Achmed (not his real name), came into the cemetery to help me. There was a strong sense in me to move down to the corner of the mural to paint. I could paint on the ground and Achmed could paint on the ladder. I spent considerable time mixing the large amounts of paint so he could paint the undercoats of colors. After a week I marveled at what we were able to accomplish. We covered the complete section of the corner to approximately 50 feet to the left. I had already begun to paint the forms and figures that would depict the triumphal entry of Jesus into Jerusalem.

CHAPTER 31

The Lamb with a Crown

Standing in front of the freshly painted background in the corner of the cemetery, it felt so good to have this section ready for details. Although the wall was still blank on my right I could look behind me and see the mural increasing in size. The beginning of the mural, the creation scene, had grown into the Noah scene, and the Abraham scenes. I had also skipped ahead for the Revelation 1:13 scenario which I planted on the back wall right at the end of the stone walkway, closer to the end of the wall. I desperately needed to feel like I was making progress. Discouragement dogged me often. I had to fight it off daily with intentionality. A glimpse of advancement gave me relief from that overwhelming feeling that I would never be able to finish it. I could breathe again.

For this section immediately past the corner of the wall, I had a very specific goal. Over a year previously, I had received in an inspiration exactly what the scene of Calvary should look like. It was crystal clear in my mind and I knew it was from the Lord. The vision depicted Jesus as the lamb going up the hill to the slaughter on the brazen altar. It also showed a Gentile, the Roman centurion decked out in the apparel of bronze armor, including a helmet and sword on the left of the lamb. On the lamb's right I saw a bearded Jewish high priest, dressed in dark long robes and head coverings. They each were looking at the innocent lamb and had a hand stretched out but were not touching him. The lamb went of his own free will to the altar of sacrifice. The Jews did not murder Christ, nor did the Gentiles. They were just the players. Jesus could have hailed a legion of angels to rescue Him. But He did no such thing. He had accepted the cup in the Garden, this was the only way, and He was the only one who qualified to provide the sacrifice of blood. This spotless lamb took the sin of the world.

Since I first received the vision for the Calvary scene, I have learned much about the reasons why the Lord did not want the traditional 'three crosses on the hill' scene. Much of the mistrust of modern Jews is from the Holocaust. Anecdotal reports verified as historical fact told of the Jews being exterminated to the routine shouts of "Christ Killers! Christ hates you!" The cross had become a symbol of terror to the Jews to the degree that they changed one of the characters of the Hebrew alphabet to remove a cross shape. I am told it is the tav. It occurred to me that had I painted the crucifixion that it may well have driven out the very people who the Lord most wanted to bless in Jerusalem. The lamb in the scene is wearing the crown of thorns. This detail leaves no guesswork as to who the lamb represents.

Since the presentation of the completed scene, we have had many types of responses and reactions to it. We have had people quickly understand the scene and others who have been perplexed. Some have literally gasped. Most fall completely silent. Some ask about the identity of the lamb. Many times Meir will question the viewers about the lamb's identity. He will tease them in a way by asking, "Where is the crucifixion?" He likes to provoke his Jewish contemporaries to think about the scene and to consider who the lamb is.

Occasionally we have a negative reaction. Someone may spit or become angry and walk away. The vast majority, however, are respectful and consider the meaning of the scene. I have had many Jewish people thank me for the sensitive portrayal of the crucifixion. What is astounding to me is that when the Lord came to me at my home in Spooner and showed me a picture of the completed mural, there were a large number of people standing in the corner and their eyes were opening. At that time I had no idea that this is the scene that would be in the view of those people looking at the mural. Now it all makes sense.

My back condition continued to heal but at least now I was painting again, my joy and resolve renewed. It took time to heal completely, even into the summer months after I returned home. I had to learn basic back care, like how to bend and how to lift.

The last session in Jerusalem was filled with contrasting experiences. There were some highs and some lows, pains and joys, yet somehow all became precious memories and I learned a lot of valuable lessons.

CHAPTER 32

Hidden Traps

Though I daily tried to give over the responsibility of the mural to the Lord, I could not help but feel the weight of the reality I faced. I was painting the Gospel of Jesus Christ, Yeshua the Messiah, in a place where there was powerful opposition to the message. Those murderous religious spirits (not people) that crucified the Lord of Glory are still alive and well on the earth. This is not about people, flesh and blood, but rather the powers and principalities of darkness in the invisible battle field that we live in. These masters of deception used people but often the people are completely unaware. The Judaizing spirit, as the Apostle Paul referred to it, visited me regularly. I learned to discern quite quickly after several years. This spiritual force would come in with a person who was oh so friendly but who had an agenda to bring you over to their way of thinking and believing. Because I am amiable, I would listen politely. The conversation would usually start innocently enough, extolling the Scriptures and the Messiah Yeshua, but would advance to say, "Yeshua is wonderful but if you really want to be close to God, observing the Torah is a true sign of love for Him. He said he didn't come to abolish the Law!"

Long before I received the invitation to paint the mural,

I had become acquainted with Jewish believers who felt that the Bible teaches that all, Jews and Gentiles, must keep the kashrut laws which are the dietary laws about food and its preparation. Their reasoning, using both Old and New Testament Scriptures, were compelling. After all, God wants us to be healthy. He has spelled out in His word certain things that are clean and some that are unclean. I had begun to consider this as something I should adhere to. I will never forget what happened next. I was about to learn a frightening but valuable lesson.

After the visit with my friends I continued to be open to this teaching of eating only biblical foods. However, I began to experience a strange phenomenon. It began with difficulty in my times in prayer. Also, I could not perceive the presence of the Lord. I was not too concerned because we all have times when we do not feel Him with our senses. But this seemed to be a dark cloud just to the left of my head. It seemed to be blocking my light in the spirit realm. It gave me a dark tight feeling. Was this my imagination? The sense of foreboding began to increase. I did not like what was happening.

I called my friend, Vicki. We go way back and I knew I could trust her with my secret. I asked if she would mind getting out her keyboard so we could praise the Lord together and take time to listen for the Lord's voice. She was eager to do this with me. She played and we began to sing out for quite some time. All the while, conscious of the dark cloud high on my left. *Suddenly a bolt of lightning, the Holy Spirit, exploded over my head.* The warm rushing flood of the presence of God came over me like a steaming shower. The dark thing was obliterated. My entire being entered a zone of holy hush. All of my body rhythms collapsed in sweet relief from the excessive tenseness caused by the pressure and fear by this blocking spirit. Then I heard Him speak to me. *"You entertained the spirit of 'another Jesus' when you failed to realize that I am enough. There is nothing more needed for your salvation. My work on the cross accomplished all. It is by faith in Me, you are saved. This is grace. I allowed the strong manifestation of this deceiving spirit so that you will learn and not be deceived."* This was only the first encounter I would experience by this religious sounding spirit who is out to take God's children on a different path. The Lord knew more lessons would be needed if I were to stay free and avoid a dangerous trap.

Paul wrote in the book of 2 Corinthians:

> *2 Co 11:3 But I fear, lest by any means, as the serpent beguiled Eve through his subtlety, so your minds should be corrupted from the simplicity that is in Christ.*
> *2 Co 11:4 For if he that comes preaching another Jesus, whom we have not preached, or if ye receive another spirit, which ye have not received, or another gospel,...*

CHAPTER 33

Opposition

Sitting quietly on a bench in the Alliance International Cemetery, on a sunny morning, I had not yet begun any painting. It was so pleasant to be there alone and just relax. Even when the vibrant green grasses wither and the ground is brown again, the tall dancing pine trees provide the touch of a forest effect. The gentle peaceful presence of God can always be detected. I heard the gate open and glanced over to see several men enter quickly, one with a larger than average camera. As one came down toward me I said hi but I don't think he heard me. There was no acknowledgment. In my thoughts I whispered a prayer: "Lord!" I immediately heard the quiet inner voice of the Holy Spirit: "Say nothing."

Most visitors enter through the gates and look around with curiosity and then begin to saunter down the long flagstone walkway. But these visitors came in as though they were on a mission with only three minutes to spy and run out. Oh, I thought, these men are looking for evidence of missionary work. As I sat still I felt quite invisible as these men walked around, took photos, and did a quick study.

Several days after this unusual visit at the cemetery, I began to feel very discouraged about the painting process. I was painting high on the wall at the time. I was up on a large scaffold near the timeline of the Israelites' long trek through the wilderness.

Standing up from my kneeling position on the concrete ledge, my body ached everywhere. I stretched my arms and took several deep breaths as the sore muscles cried in protest. I looked at the long blank wall waiting for the mural to be formed and birthed. How can I really paint this whole wall? This is too much for me. At first I did not perceive the mental bombardment as anything but my own thoughts. But then the storm began to escalate. "There is so much I have to do to even put the brush on the wall. Every time I come there are funds to gather so I can travel again. I never know if I will have enough. Lodging has to be reserved in advance each time I come. Finding a place is not so easy. The average rent for a short term stay is over one thousand dollars a month just for an efficiency apartment." The negative thought pattern ramped up and redoubled its efforts to bring me down into a pit. Then there was the situation at home of my daughter, a single parent, and my granddaughter and all of the concerns any normal mother would carry. I needed my husband. Overlaid onto all of these pressing matters was the constant companion of random but regular terror attacks in the city. There was a deep grief that would envelop Jerusalem every time a person died in one of these attacks. It was a sadness mingled with utter frustration at the injustice the victims' families had to face and the knowledge of their gaping loss. On and on went the loop in my brain.

We all have worries that center around our security and loved ones, but when they come all at once in an unrelenting onslaught, you can be sure it is a well-orchestrated purposeful attack against us by our chief adversary. I would love to tell you that I was so strong and triumphed quickly but such was not the case. I was weary from weeks of the painting regimen. My defenses were weak and I did not recognize immediately what was really happening. A tight cloud of depression came over me and I was discouraged to the point of tears. Even breathing seemed difficult. Feeling like I could not go on, I began to entertain thoughts of going home to the US. The swirling thoughts were taking me under like someone floundering in the ocean. "This vision to paint a very large mural of the Bible was just not possible in this tumultuous environment," I pondered. I wanted to go home.

One of those sunless days, I called a friend who was in ministry in Jerusalem. She was full of the Spirit and a kindred heart as well. When I poured out my woes to Marylois, she zeroed into the very epicenter of the fiery trial I was experiencing. "This is a spiritual battle. What you are doing is of great value to God. It is time to call out the intercessors to pray. Perhaps you should have people right there with you praying while you paint." This struck a chord in my spirit.

God speaks to his children in many ways. The next week I was making plans to change my airline reservation to leave a few weeks early. During that week, a lovely Jewish lady, a believer who lives in Israel, came in to see the mural. She marveled and was very animatedly telling me how important the mural would be to many people. She then spoke almost the same words as my friend on the phone that day. My spirit leapt at the recognition of my Lord's loving direction. I needed help. It was time to call out the troops.

It was quite a while before we connected the dots of this attack with the visitors who so roughly entered the gates the previous week. Was there a correlation? Were there psychic powers being released against the mural and the mural painter? Perhaps it was demonic minions from the one who is leading the world into denial of the true living God and the Son He sent.

The primary cause for my persistence in the face of the constant stress in the mural painting process was my grateful heart to Yeshua. The years of darkness and then the struggle to be free were badges of love and honor from the One who went before me. Because He spoke to me in such a personal way there was no doubt in my mind that painting the mural was His calling on my life. I felt like my entire existence was a grand life lesson so I could succeed in doing this one thing for Him. So when troubles came, it was not easy, yet I knew He would help me every step of the way. I had to learn to rely on Him in ways I had never imagined. As trouble came so consistently, I had to recognize that the enemy was very real and the attacks were designed to destroy my soul and my faith.

The spring session of 2012 was a difficult, fiery time for me. I grabbed a flight home two and a half weeks earlier than planned and knew it was the right thing to do. I was suffering burn-out due to the constant draining battle.

My family and friends usually gave me much grace and solitude knowing I was in a recovery mode for about ten days after I returned to Spooner. If I were to be hooked up to a heart monitor, it would be a flatline with an occasional bump, just enough to know I was still alive. When strength came sufficiently to leave the house, I would go with Carl to our various services at our home church. These dear warrior saints would pray over me and help bring me back to life. Honesty is always the best policy so I would tell them about the struggles and what led to the condition I presented. Lots of cleansing tears would flow. The many pairs of comforting strong arms of love around me helped considerably as well.

It was amazing to me how God would supply my need for love. I seemed to need more love than the average person. Was it my imagination or did I have more trials than the average Christian? Isolating myself from people was one of my 'things' back in the day, but now I seemed to flow in love for other people. It was not difficult for me. I see them with the eyes of one who is loved. But I also needed a lot of love. When my love tank was low, the Lord would pour into me. He used the people who supported me and who shared the vision of the mural to supply my greatest need. Pastor John from my church led the way because, of course, I was there the most. These believers are kindred spirits. Full of the Spirit but very 'down to earth,' I knew I could be real with these people. The people from my former church, the Shell Lake Full Gospel, always reached out to me too.

There was another church which persisted in loving me through thick and thin during the mural painting process and it was the Calvary Lutheran Church from Lee, Illinois. Pastor Craig and wife Barb had become close friends when they still lived in our area in 'up north' Wisconsin. Craig was part of the original prayer meetings that I initiated in 2002. When I could no longer attend regularly because of my work obligations, he assumed the leadership. His big heart of love for the Jews ached over the anti-Semitism he witnessed in elements of the Lutheran church. He did his best to correct and teach what the Bible says about the land of Israel and the chosen people. When Pastor Craig and Barb moved to Illinois, he set the stage for me to come and to talk to his congregation repeatedly, about my call to Israel and my involvement with the Jewish people. I visited once and sometimes twice each year. The people of this church truly 'caught the vision' of the mural in Jerusalem and not only loved me but supplied thousands of dollars during the six and a half years of painting to help the mural toward completion. Roger K. and his wife Kathleen and son Kristian were members at the time who helped me to rent our first apartment in Jerusalem. They always freely gave of their bounty to help the mural move forward. Their enthusiasm for the mural and their love for Israel was astounding to me. Without the love and support of these believers and all those who loved me unconditionally and helped me along the way, this huge job would have been impossible. The Lord connected all of our lives through these challenging years. When Kathleen died due to cancer, it was a great loss to all. When we love much, we also hurt much. The two go hand in hand. When Dr. John, from the congregation in Illinois, came to visit in Jerusalem, together we painted one of the birds Kathleen loved, a cardinal, on the mural in her honor. Our lives are interwoven forever; the love we share does not fade.

One year after the mural was completed, Pastor Craig was diagnosed with brain cancer. We were stunned and sad. Although we prayed for healing, Craig died and is sorely missed. However, Craig and Barb were able to experience Israel before he died. I had the privilege of escorting them through the land. When Pastor Craig saw the mural with his own eyes, he was touched by God's Spirit. The love and support that he gave to me, to Israel and to the people of Israel all those years, will never be forgotten. The Alliance Church recognized his contributions by wholeheartedly accepting his ashes into the Alliance International Cemetery for burial. Now we can tell Pastor Craig's story to our visitors, his legacy of love continues.

CHAPTER 34

Mosaic of Volunteers

The following session, fall of 2012, marked the beginning of the season of intercessors. The Holy Spirit had impressed upon me that I must not put even one stroke on the mural without at least one person praying. The person had to be with me in the cemetery. Painting the Gospel message in the heart of Jerusalem for all to see was not popular with the devil and those who desired the darkness rather than the light. It was so encouraging to have this mandate. The Lord began to supply the need. One by one or two by two, various individuals became stirred to come to Jerusalem. Most were friends but some were soon to be friends; plus, most had never before been to Israel. This new door was instrumental in bringing a literal 'revival' into the lives of those He touched to come and pray. The new door led to the building of a bridge that each person would walk over safely to come to Israel and participate in this miracle. Some eventually would walk back and forth many times.

It takes faith to come to Israel. The Middle East is portrayed by the media as a place of instability and terrorism. Israel is actually very safe. But the presentation by many media sources can leave people who want to come battling fear in their minds. Leaving the comfort of consistent home life in America and coming across the ocean is something many will never do. Thankfully, God had been preparing people to get out of the boat like Peter did and to walk on the water by faith in the unfailing love of a faithful God.

The connection with key intercessors began late that summer of 2011, when there was a tent revival-type meeting in my neighborhood in the Spooner area. Among the praise and worship team members from the Twin Cities area was Scott S., a guitar player. I remember meeting him and talking with him a little. He said he would be coming to Jerusalem in the fall, first with a Christian tour group and then he would be staying for a while. He felt very much called by the Lord to be there. What I did not realize at the time was that this brother-in-the-faith was really, really called—not only called to be in Israel but to be an integral and long term part of the newly formed mural team of prayer and worship.

Scott was a young man even though he was in his fifties. His continuous jokes and lighthearted attitude, along with his clean cut features, gave him a youthful appearance and made it a pleasure to have him in our company. He always wore a panama hat that would be more accurately described as a safari hat. Scott with his hat and guitar would prove a popular figure with the locals in Jerusalem.

Scott was rescued from the darkness and from an addiction to alcohol, two divorces, and brought into the glorious light of Yeshua. His grateful heart is expressed through his music and a lifestyle that reflect his Rescuer. He is dependable and a passionate God-lover like me. He was and is filled with the Holy Spirit and is very sensitive to the spiritual temperature of the atmosphere. These attributes brought a security to our operations in the cemetery against the schemes of the adversary. Especially the times when Carl could not be present, here was a man that could be trusted to be true and righteous.

Scott also yielded to my requests to model when I needed a certain pose for the mural scenes. When it was time to paint the hand of the shepherd who came to worship baby Jesus in the manger, I shouted "Sco-o-o-o-t! I need your hand!" Scott was strolling with his guitar, lost in prayerful reverie amid the gently swaying pines. The cemetery dimensions are long and narrow. The long wall is approximately 350 feet or 90 meters. The short side is approximately 170 feet. It is quite a large space. If I needed to speak to someone on the other end, they might not be able to hear even if I called loudly.

It could be quite comical when Scott would oblige me and sometimes have to pose like a pretzel to accommodate the effect that I needed for a particular scene. He would always make me laugh with his quips and puns. This was so therapeutic for me. I could become much too serious.

In the fall of 2012, the parade of short term prayer volunteers began. Dayle was a friend for many years who lived only two and a half miles from my place. We were prayer partners, walking partners and confidants. She did not think it possible for her to come and help pray at the mural, although it was a desire she had. She did not think her husband would ever agree with her to leave rural Wisconsin to come to a foreign country. But she was oh so wrong. She nearly fainted on the day her husband asked her why she was not going to go help her friend in Israel. This was all the urging she needed and promptly made plans to come. Dayle was a great help. She was delighted to experience a new culture and to be among the Jewish people. She relished her opportunity to love the people and be able to assist the creation of the mural through her prayer watch. She came twice and, afterward, she took her firsthand knowledge of the situation in Israel and her love for the people back home and continued a prayer ministry for Israel.

Nona and Brenda from the Dakotas, whom I had not

known previously, came highly recommended through other friends and supporters like Barbara H. I was a part of Barbara's nonprofit ministry organization for a few years. Barbara saw the value in what I was doing and offered her help. I received Barbara's recommendations with confidence. Brenda and Nona truly stepped into the prayer role with diligence. We lived together in an apartment building in Arnona on the edge of Jerusalem. We were on the fourth floor of a place that had two bedroom suites. Each room had its own bathroom. This situation worked very well. They became wonderful friends.

The people who interrupted their normal lives to come and help are, without exception, overcomers as much as I am. They have lived through lives of adversity and pain. They are people of faith who are tried and tested, once broken but now healed. They came with a motivation of pure love to be involved in something greater than themselves.

CHAPTER 35

Surprise in the Sky

The organic and unpredictable way of life in Jerusalem will definitely keep you on your knees. It is a place where a simple task such as grocery shopping can take up the whole day. It does not help that life in Israel includes dealing with violent acts like car rammings and stabbings of civilians. A person must tread carefully, knowing where to go and where to avoid. The threat of imminent war is also on the minds of most people in Israel. In fact, for several mural painting sessions I was advised by friends here to take gas masks along with me. There was a lot of talk about the possibility of biological warfare coming against the citizens of Israel. But in 2012, over 1,456 Kassam and Grad rockets were fired into mostly southern Israel between November 14 and 21. Even Jerusalem was targeted. Israelis everywhere were running for safety for the first time since the first Gulf War 20 years ago. Depending on where they lived and how close they were to the launch of the rockets, they would have anywhere from 13 seconds to 60 seconds to get in the shelters. The Operation Pillar of Defense was the military action that took place in response to this deluge.

Dolean and another friend, Cheryl, were planning to come and be my prayer partners for a few weeks. Of course, they heard the frightening reports about the rocket fire. At that point the only places getting rockets were closer to Sderot, who got most of them. Cheryl is a school teacher so it was not easy to get a substitute teacher for this time period. When the door opened she felt sure the Holy Spirit was leading her. Her family was concerned for her welfare. The day before her flight, she emailed to say she was coming despite the threats. I replied encouraging her to trust the Lord and come. I reassured her for her family's sake that there were no rockets landing anywhere near us in Jerusalem and that it had been many years since anything had happened there.

That very evening, which was a Friday, Erev Shabbat, I had just returned to my apartment on the fourth floor in the big complex in Arnona after a full day of visitors at the cemetery. I had opened the glass door to the small balcony. I loved being up and seeing the everyday activity of the neighborhood and the blue sky as well. Just as I took a deep breath, a piercing and haunting sound filled my ears and startled my heart. Multiple sirens of different pitches were sounding in eerie harmony. I had never heard sirens like that before. As I looked down and saw Israelis begin to run, the reality hit me like a ton of bricks. Israelis don't run. They take their time unless there is a life threatening situation at hand. *This must be an alert for a rocket attack.* I grabbed my cell phone and called the apartment manager. As I queried him about the sirens, he calmly told me that the sounds I was hearing were indeed a warning that a rocket had been fired into Jerusalem airspace. "Go into your bedroom and close the door. It is a bomb shelter," he said. My heart raced instantly as I grabbed my water bottle and a banana. Before I entered my bedroom I stepped onto the balcony once more. Curiosity was getting the better of me. I heard and felt a deep reverberating thud. It sounded a ways away, yet the immensity of this sound was formidable. "Was that the sound of the rocket exploding into the earth?" I wondered.

Not having experienced anything like this in my life to this point, I did not know what to expect. Were there going to be more rockets, more sirens? I sat on my bed and prayed. Silence prevailed. After approximately 30 minutes and still no other warnings, I decided to take my chances and exit the heavy door of my bedroom bomb shelter. When I turned the big latch, the door did not open. I tried it again and again. I could not get the door open. I could not get out! A panic struck my mind. My apartment door was locked and no one could get in here, even if someone heard me banging on the door. An uninvited scenario of me hanging out the fourth floor window yelling to be rescued flashed in my mind. "Wait! Is there a cell signal?" Thankfully I had my cell phone and surprisingly there was a signal even in this armored room. I called my landlord and told him I was trapped in the bomb shelter. *"Patricia, I am sorry but I am not in the city, I cannot come to help you right now."* He proceeded to give me ideas on how to open the door with the big lever-style handle. At first nothing seemed to be helping. But with my fifth or sixth attempt, as I pushed with all of my body strength, cranked the lever, and prayed, *snap*! The sound of heavy metal popping in movement was music to my ears! The door opened up. This experience of being locked inside the shelter was more terrifying than the rockets themselves. I told my landlord I was out and we laughed together in relief! He seems to find humor in reminding me often of my imprisonment. But I don't mind. We laugh all over again.

Cheryl and Dolean were in the skies over the Atlantic by the time Jerusalem had its rocket attack. "Oops," I thought. "How was I supposed to know this would happen?" Truly the Lord was with them, bringing them to Jerusalem for His purpose. They were safe in His arms.

There was another rocket attack that same week. Dolean

and Cheryl had gone on a tour to Bethlehem. Scott and I had just finished up at the mural and were walking on Emek Rephaim Street when the harmonic sirens sounded the alarm of an approaching rocket. We looked at each other and said at the same time, "Back to the cemetery!" Because there was a semblance of protection to the walls we reasoned this would be better than on the streets. We quickly opened the concrete shed door and then closed it just as quickly when we realized there were many potential projectiles inside, like shovels, pitch forks, and other assorted blades, should the rocket land near and shake the ground. We decided that the newly built wooden scaffold next to the stone wall could be a better place. Scott was, of course, finding great humor in visualizing a mass resurrection of people buried in the cemetery if a rocket were to land in the midst of the graves. We had barely sat down when we heard that resounding boom once again. Indeed it was the rocket hitting the earth. We found later that it landed between us and Bethlehem, which is only about six miles toward the south. Living through a couple of rocket attacks in Jerusalem gives one an intimate peek into the life of the people of Israel. We must remember when we read all of the political outrage at Israel being here in the land, that most Jewish people live here because of something much deeper and much more compelling than logic or current affairs. The Bible foretold long ago that the Lord would bring His dispersed people back to the land He gave them through Abraham, Isaac, and Jacob. It really defies logical thinking to bring your family to some place where the neighbors want to get rid of you. I care about the Palestinian people. However, the extremist elements have radicalized many of the people. There are Arabs who do not agree with the violent methods but they are forced to be silent due to life-threatening control of the leaders over the people. Many secretly want to go back to more peaceful times of working side by side in relative prosperity. I have personally spoken to some of these Arab people. I especially care about their young men who are brought up in a culture of hate. Many have no hope for a life outside of hatred of the Jews. They are manipulated to commit suicide by attacking Jews and they are called martyrs. When I see them on the street I want to cry for them. I wish I could start a scholarship program to help them to be able to go elsewhere and discover that there is good in this world. Wouldn't it be wonderful for the young men to have hope and to know it is possible to have a future?

CHAPTER 36

Foreshadow of Trouble

The 2012 fall mural painting session was filled with a kaleidoscope of people and events that caused it to have a special place in my mural memories. We had two unexpected volunteers from America who proved to be dear as well as valuable to us. George had roots in my town in Wisconsin and Vince was and is his pastor from Arkansas. They dove right into the many tasks large and small that went into the mural. They navigated the scaffold and painted the background for the scene of the prophets and kings. This meant having to work on the ledge, which is about seven feet up. George was 80 years young at the time but could leap around that ledge and scaffold like a boy.

George spent quite a bit of time with us, including our prayer and worship times. Campaigns for the next US president were in high gear in America. The six of us who had gathered were all passionate about praying over our nation. We unfolded the American flag that we kept in the shed. We prayed and some wept over the United States of America. It was a sad and tragic time in the US as the portal to hell was opened in so many ways, affecting even our school children and what they were taught about right and wrong and the foundational truths that shaped our nation.

As several of us sat together at our familiar corner pouring out our hearts in prayer, there was another issue laying heavily on my heart. I had not told others about this concern because I was hoping it would cease to be a problem. My husband, who still worked full time as a licensed social worker for Burnett County, was back home and experiencing a mysterious infection. He had surgery in 2002 for prostate cancer but had no further incidents as such. As were many Vietnam veterans, he was on the Agent Orange list due to exposure to the toxic herbicides used during his 12 month tour there. Several rounds of meds failed to arrest this nagging condition. That lurking fear that the cancer could return is a realistic burden for survivors of cancer and spouses, I might add. I decided to bring it out into the open so others could pray with me about this worry. George took up request to pray for Carl. As I heard my hidden fear spoken out in this prayer of faith, my spirit shuddered. My silent tears revealed the depth of my apprehension.

Arriving home in early December, I was able to accompany Carl to several appointments at the Minneapolis VA as the doctors pursued an explanation for the persistent infection. With each passing week, we both grew more concerned, yet trusting, believing for the best—always giving the weight of our burden over to Jesus. We had no way of knowing the difficult path that lie ahead for us. But there is One who knew what was looming in the near future. He sent a special messenger ahead with a message for us, so our faith would not be shaken in the trying days to come.

When I was still in Jerusalem painting away, an unfamiliar figure walked through the gates one cool and breezy November morning. This was not unusual in itself, yet something about this man grabbed my attention. I had no interest in breaking my concentration so kept on with the job at hand. But he lingered for a time and then approached me. His name was Nathaniel (not his real name), from the UK. He began to extol the Lord Jesus and speak about the mural in such a personal way I knew it was the LORD speaking. He said, *"Even as Mary poured the precious oil from the Alabaster box onto Jesus, that my 'brokenness' is being poured out as worship unto Jesus as I paint the mural and that this anointing would bring life to those who would behold it."* His words gave voice to something that was deep in my heart and was the essence of my motivation to paint the mural. He spoke so eloquently of that which I already felt; that the mural is my worship unto the Lord. Now it was clear that Nathaniel was prophesying. He spoke about my past pain being a preparation to be able to pour out love made exquisite through suffering and faithfulness. He continued to speak as I clicked on my phone's recording app. Then he dropped a bombshell: Nathaniel said that the Lord was going to heal my husband completely and that he would not have anything wrong with him. He even prophesied about my husband's retirement and spoke of our new life together. I was slightly stunned to have this clear and succinct window to our future, especially in light of the present concerns about Carl's health. I pondered it often over the next six months.

This time of my life was intricately woven into the fabric of my paintings. The rending of my heart for my husband's dark time produced a hemorrhage of pain, certainly, but also of love—a growing love inside my being that was rooted in the transformation of who I was and who I was becoming, no matter what life threw at me. This love was not based on whim or emotion but a passion from a passionate God who was living inside His holy temple.

The medical diagnostics included biopsies and some minor surgery. The next week Carl and I were called in for a consultation. The urologist informed us that they had found bladder cancer, but did not know how extensive. More testing that day revealed no other cancer. They believed it was contained in the bladder. However, two days before Christmas, we were told that the bladder and prostate would need to be removed because of medical realities and statistical evidence that diminished his chances of long term survival. They were also prescribing chemotherapy before the surgery.

A mixed bag of emotions assailed our minds and hearts. Deflated and quiet, we prayed together during the two hour and forty five minute drive home from Minneapolis to Spooner. Sober, meditative, somber, stricken, yet somehow courageous, are all descriptors of this painful event that this married couple had to process following the report. We prayed every day for a miracle reversal, yet we knew that our lives are His and our God would be in this with us. Our Lord, who knows what pain is and who knows what death is all about—this Lord who was tempted in all points human yet prevailed—this God would take our hand and guide us through the maze of fear, faith, hope, and love.

Of all the incredible life lessons we receive along our way, there is none as valuable as learning to take one day at a time, in my opinion. I am more of a visionary by nature, so this truth was not easy for me. But now with the overwhelming and threatening situation of my husband having life-threatening cancer, I had to learn this one-day-at-a-time drill for sheer survival. One of my best teachers of this lesson is a woman who became my friend in more recent years. She is the wife of the retired pastor, Milt, at our church. She had suffered from cardiovascular disease for several years and had to learn to live on the edge of life with constant reminders of her mortality. She was very sympathetic toward my situation and reached out to me frequently. She would tell me I did not have to be strong and to let Jesus be my strength. I would call her from the VA during our many trips for chemo and other medical procedures feeling overwhelmed, hurting for Carl. She would tell me, "It is okay to cry." Cry I did, letting out all of the pressure and woes. She would just *be* with me at those moments. I felt so cherished knowing that my Abba Father had put this special love in Myrna's for this special time of great need.

Carl is a man's man. "Once a Marine, always a Marine," it is said of these former soldiers. He is also a hunter and a sharp shooter, a builder, and an avid sports fan. Carl knows all the who's who in the political world. He could have run for president. He has a more plausible political ideology than the best of the politicians. He is one smart guy with wisdom to boot. His favorite aspect of manhood has been and I think will always be, being a father. He loves his kids and grandkids. He would do anything for them. He insists they know they are loved and that we believe in them. Against the odds that Vietnam veterans face, he overcame PTSD to become a loving husband and dad. He is one of the real unsung heroes of his generation. It is Carl who empowered me to keep going back to Israel and to keep painting in the face of obstacles and exhaustion. His quiet strength is always evident. We all know it is difficult to see our loved ones in any kind of pain, but seeing my big strong, he-man husband diminish physically right before my eyes, knowing he was powerless to do anything about it—that is a killer.

The deepest and darkest valley of this entire trial occurred when we received the copy of Carl's medical records that he requested. The documents included the diagnostic terminology and name of the cancer he was facing. As we usually do, we decided to do a little research for ourselves and did some digging to find out more about this particular type of cancer. As we read the results of our search, a tangible horror struck us simultaneously. Even with radical surgery and chemotherapy the prognosis was only about three to six months of life. We were horrified and crushed. We could barely speak. Our hopes and faith were dashed upon the rocks of medical statistics. We couldn't even look at each other for fear of completely losing composure. As in slow motion, we each withdrew to our silent corners to get our bearings.

It really did not help matters when, at the VA for Carl's chemo treatment, a woman in the commissary with whom I had struck up a conversation, told me that her husband had just passed away from the identical type of cancer that Carl had been diagnosed with. I heard myself yell inside, "No! I do not want to hear this!" But now quietly I prayed, *"Lord, please tell me you are* ***not*** *preparing me to lose Carl."*

On Tuesday afternoon I went to our regular prayer meeting for Israel. I had not really wanted to go to the prayer meeting. Discouragement hung on me like an old winter coat. Carl was not feeling good and decided to stay home. Somehow I managed to put one foot in front of the other and then drove north to the church. After our initial prayers, Pastor John knew I was in the pit and asked if he could pray for me. Sure, why not? I have never been able to hide my feelings very well, not that I had to hide them, but it was a part of me to be real. I couldn't help it. I was down and it showed. As he placed his hand gently on my head, I heard him praying. I was not really paying attention; I felt like nothing could really move me back to faith. But after about two minutes, I started to feel something—it was the presence of God! I slowly became charged with the Holy Spirit. Something like hope…and faith entered my spirit. I leapt to my feet and started thanking and praising the Lord in a loud trembling voice. Everyone in the room felt it too, and responded in kind. *Then I saw it*—in the spirit, I saw a picture in full color and motion. I saw a surging waterfall like the Niagara, roaring and crashing down. It signified '*breakthrough*!' The waterfall scene then parted like a stage curtain and opened up. There I saw Carl and I, holding hands and walking down Emek Rephaim Street in Jerusalem. Wow, this is our future! I believed with all of my heart that the Lord was revealing to me that Carl would not only live through this ordeal but would again go to Jerusalem with me. I was sobbing, releasing all of the pent up emotion and fear of losing my husband. Everything inside of me came up from the deep. Then I heard the words of a scripture being read by Denny, one of our elders. It was Zephaniah.

> *Zep 3:14 Sing, O daughter of Zion; shout, O Israel; be glad and rejoice with all the heart, O daughter of Jerusalem. The LORD hath taken away thy judgments, he hath cast out thine enemy: the king of Israel, even the LORD, is in the midst of thee: thou shalt not see evil any more In that day it shall be said to Jerusalem, Fear thou not: and to Zion, Let not thine hands be slack. The LORD thy God in the midst of thee is mighty; he will save, he will rejoice over thee with joy; he will rest in his love, he will joy over thee with singing. I will gather them that are sorrowful for the solemn assembly, who are of thee, to whom the reproach of it was a burden. Behold, at that time I will undo all that afflict thee: and I will save her that halts, and gather her that was driven out; and I will get them praise and fame in every land where they have been put to shame. At that time will I bring you again, even in the time that I gather you: for I will make you a name and a praise among all people of*

the earth, when I turn back your captivity before your eyes, saith the LORD.

Beyond any doubt, I knew that this was my God speaking His Word of life to me! The realization of what just happened lifted my heart into a realm of fresh hope and wonderment. That the Lord would reach into my world in this way to comfort and speak comfort and hope to me is beyond natural comprehension. The inner picture of Carl and I walking hand in hand in Jerusalem became my constant companion.

Bladder cancer requires chemotherapy prior to surgical removal in order to give more assurance that all the cancer cells are eradicated. Every two weeks we traveled to the Minneapolis VA Center for the chemo treatments. Carl's body handled them well. This was quite remarkable as we were told the strength of the chemo was the strongest dose a human body can sustain without killing it. Carl sailed through, and we were both amazed—that is, until the final chemo treatment. Carl did not seem to lose his strength throughout this process. He would need to rest more than usual in between appointments but in general he felt good. This last dose however, hit him like a Mack truck. He did not bounce back after this one. Even the doctor was a bit concerned if he possessed the strength for the surgical ordeal he would have to face. More prayer, more trusting, more prayer requests for our God family.

May 11, 2013 Carl underwent radical surgery. He was admitted the day prior to the scheduled event. He seemed more quiet than usual. The day of the surgery many friends and family were praying. This was so encouraging to know.

As Carl lay quietly on his hospital bed, waiting for all of the procedural preparations to be completed, some friends called and we prayed together for a long time. It was a brother in the faith who is a Messianic Rabbi and his wife.

They hold a special place in my heart. They have given their encouragement and loving support to us throughout the mural painting years. I relish times of prayer that are soft and slow. Those prayers that capture the need so poetically are a comfort in themselves, knowing the God who knows all, inspired even the words. The four of us prayed and lingered.

Afterward the call was over, Carl was able to express his deepest fear that he would not come out of the surgery. I am not sure why this surprised me, but he had given no indication of having to deal with this. Surely I could understand it; anyone could. Pangs of love and sorrow touched my emotions as I saw my best friend, my soulmate, my lover, in this vulnerable state. All I could do was keep squeezing his hand and telling him how much I loved him.

To my surprise and delight, Myrna called early in the day to say that she and Bonnie were coming to be with me. Myrna had barely been able to leave her house for months because of her physical condition, but today, love compelled her to go by faith. I was so happy and honored, and humbled, too, in a way. None of our kids could be there due to jobs or other pressing situations. They wanted to be but it just wasn't possible. This compensated nicely.

The time arrived for Carl to meet with the anesthesiologist and I had to leave the room. The head of the surgical team then found me. He said he would be in communication with me on a regular basis. He gave me a number to dial if I had questions or concerns. He was professional and confident but also warm. He estimated the complicated surgery to be five hours in length.

As the big 'wait' began, the three of us, Myrna, Bonnie and I, began with a time of prayer. It was so nice to not be alone. After the peace of God had buoyed our hearts, we had time to visit and enjoy some light-hearted banter. I received calls from the surgical team about every hour and was reassured that all was well. The pressure mounted, however, when the five-hour mark had passed. Neither were there phone calls from the medical team. Beating back panic, I called to remembrance the life-giving words of Nathaniel the believer from the UK. "Carl will be healed!" I also forced myself to think about the astounding intervention during prayer time a few months previous during Israel prayer in Pastor John's office.

Another call came in from one of the doctors. The surgeons had encountered a complication that they had not anticipated. On Carl's insides there was a fusion of some of his inner organs due to the radiation therapy he had received when he first had cancer in 2002. This made it difficult for the current surgeon to perform his job to extricate the bladder. It was glued in and it took more time and cutting which led to more bleeding and the need for transfusions. It was nine hours before the final call came. He was out of surgery and in recovery. He had received six units of blood.

I was numb. I think Myrna and Bonnie were as well. The surgery was more complicated than they had expected. I had to wait another hour before I was allowed into the recovery ICU. When I saw him, he was very groggy, but his eyes were open. I cried. He wept, too. He said, "I feel pain and that is a good thing. It means that I made it. I'm still alive!" I knew he would not remember any of our conversation later as he was still quite out of it. With a great sense of relief and thanksgiving, I sat down to wait again, but now it was a lot easier. Our son, Sean, was able to come up later. What comfort to see his loving face, he is much like his dad, and get that strong embrace. Being with him was like a salve that soothed the rough edges of the day.

Modern medicine is truly remarkable. These medical geniuses were able to craft a new body part from a part of Carl's intestines that would now suffice for the elimination of urine from his body. He would soon receive an education from the nurses that would make his life without a bladder, do-able. The healing and adjustment phase of Carl's recovery would be lengthy. This we were prepared for.

Ten days after surgery Carl still could not eat *any* food and we became alarmed. The extensive nature of the procedure resulted in a shutdown of his digestive function. It refused to resume its duties. "How is Carl going to heal without nutrition?" was my question. Eventually a PICC line was inserted and he was able to have nourishment.

Eating was not happening, and moving was also difficult. Carl was very weak. At one point during this testy time, the doctor came in and told Carl that he had to force himself to walk, even if just a few steps at a time. He explained that as he attempted mobility he was delivering a potent message to all of his bodily systems. The message: "You are needed. I am alive and *you will function.*" I had not heard of this but it made perfect sense to me, and to Carl also. Every day they brought light food for him to try, but he couldn't do it. If he managed to force himself, it all came back up.

The hospital ward was another problem. The staff was efficient and friendly but the environment was frenzied with the constant action, people with carts in and out. The noises, whether it was people talking near or far, or body sounds of all kinds from the other three patients in the room; it was never quiet. Carl decided he would heal a lot better at home. He outright lied to the nurses saying he had started eating. He was discharged after 22 days.

As Carl settled in at home, he began to improve almost immediately. I made his meals mostly with eggs. The doctor had recommended eggs. They were easy on his ravaged system and he liked eggs. Carl's healing was in progress. His digestive system decided it was okay to live again and began to function. "Oh thank you Lord!" Yes, the Lord was with us every step, every day in every way. This was the only season of painting I missed in the six and a half years of mural painting.

What can be said about this time of upheaval that invaded our lives like a rampaging bull? We made it through. There has been a steady flow of thanksgiving emerging from my heart ever since—more than I have ever known myself to have. Carl is thankful as well, however, he now has to deal with the loss of his bladder every day. It is a major inconvenience, but still minor in comparison to the alternative. He complains about it, and he has a right to do it. By the fall of 2013, Carl was getting much stronger and felt he could manage just fine without me for a couple of months. "Honey, you need to go back to Jerusalem. Keep painting!" What a guy!

One year after his radical surgery, Carl and I were in the German Colony of Jerusalem, on Emek Rephaim Street, approaching the gates of the Alliance International Cemetery, holding hands, and laughing. I reminded Carl about the words of the man who was sent to give us hope and about the vision of the waterfall. Here we were literally living the vision, holding hands on Emek Rephaim Street. We fell into a holy hush as we reflected on all that had taken place. Then we laughed.

CHAPTER 37

Blessed on the Mountains Are Our Feet

The fall of 2013, I returned to Jerusalem with two of my best friends from home. Carl was doing well and continuing to heal. He had urged me to return to work on the mural. As I prepared to travel, I felt like I had sprouted wings. Even before my feet lifted off from American soil, I was soaring.

It was always so amazing to me that no matter who came alongside to help the mural become a reality, each person brought something uniquely theirs to bless Israel and the people of Israel. Bonnie had brought her recorder along. During our frequent praise and worship times, she discovered a flow of spontaneous notes that seemed to travel out of the cemetery even into the streets of the German Colony. She would begin to play in synchrony with Scott on his guitar. It was captivating. I think the host of heaven came to attention at the sound of these spontaneous melodies. Majel played the Djembe drum, which added a lively rhythm to our music. But Majel's true calling and gift is in teaching the Bible. She was a serious student of the Bible. God called this gift out of His treasury in a unique experience a little later on.

After a couple of weeks in the cemetery, Majel, Bonnie, and I decided to escape the rigors of life in Jerusalem in exchange for the rigors of life in northern Israel for a couple of days. I wanted to show them the most breathtaking vista I had ever seen in my life. It happened to be at a kibbutz guesthouse on the northern border of Israel. I had been there several times in the past and I was in awe every time. The lush greenery was a stark contrast to the rocky desert tones in central and south Israel. Here at the tippy top of the country were high mountains that seemed to slant in perpendicular fashion to the earth. The tilt of the land forms almost gave me vertigo and aided in creating a surrealistic feeling of one foot in heaven. When nighttime came, it dropped like a heavy velvet curtain and suddenly a million lights from many villages were shimmering in the steel blue dusk of the Hula Valley. It was absolutely hypnotic.

As we arrived and settled into our rustic accommodations, we noticed a flyer on the coffee table telling of a tour given by two local men who were Israeli war veterans. We agreed it could be fun and educational so I called and spoke with a man named Baruch (not his real name). He clearly had a rough but charming personality in an Israeli way and invited us to take part in their tour the next day.

We were the only takers for the short tour and soon the lecture began with a man named Avi. Both men were in their sixties and seasoned in everything Israeli. They were very friendly and seemed happy to have Americans to entertain. They told us about border life and the dangers that were poised to threaten Israel just a few kilometers across the valley. Avi continued to speak about many topics, politics, and the weather. He even boasted about how many Christians they served and how well they got along. As I began to visit with Baruch, who was an artist and sculptor, I overheard Avi say in a brassy voice, "We like the Christians but I don't need Jesus, He is for the Gentiles." Duly noted, I continued my conversation with the other guy about art when I heard almost the same phrase repeated by Avi. As he continued speaking with Majel, for the third time, he said, "Because I am a Jew, I do not need Jesus." My soul prayed instantly, "O Lord, You heard this?!" My prayer had barely escaped my heart when without any warning, I beheld my dear friend, Majel, sweet, and petite, so soft spoken, put out her dainty index finger, aiming it at his face, utter with all the authority of heaven, *"But in your Bible it is written that the Messiah will come sitting on a donkey, just like Jesus did when he entered Jerusalem."* "Oh no," retorted Avi. "That is in the Christian Bible." "Not so," Majel countered. "It is found in the book of Zechariah in the ninth chapter. And did you know that it is foretold that there will be a wicked ruler, the Antichrist, who will rise up to rule the world and that you will be tricked by him, at first?" Majel began to quote the book of Daniel. Avi countered: "Not me, I won't be tricked, ha, you have warned me." On and on they went, a duel of eternal consequence. It was a sight to behold as this sweet lady brought out her secret weapon—knowledge of the Holy Scriptures. She spoke the Scriptures in a way that Avi could not refute. It was like listening to God the Father reasoning with a son. When Bonnie had heard this unusual conversation taking place she moved to a quiet corner and immediately began to pray and intercede for this man.

My conversation took an unexpected turn as well. Baruch began to confess some things that he had done in his life and was ashamed of. I didn't hesitate to share my story with him about forgiveness. I was surprised by his openness with me. I knew the Lord was doing something. Baruch took me into a different shop and showed off some of his sculptures. Now I could see clearly that he was a practitioner of New Age spirituality. I was gentle but I did not hold back the truth about the true and holy power of the Holy Spirit and the counterfeit powers.

As our conversations diminished, we checked the time

and realized we needed to begin the long drive back to Jerusalem. As we prepared to depart, both men were trying to give us things. They wanted to serve us somehow, they offered free drinks from the little stand, and gave us free T-shirts. This outpouring of affection just confirmed that they received something… not from us, but from the God of Israel who is passionately in love with them. As we traveled down the mountain road, we had a sense that heaven came to earth. "I think we caused an earthquake," I said as we sat quietly for a long time in the afterglow.

CHAPTER 38

The Bridge from Spooner to Jerusalem

Gene and Lila from Missouri came that session, too. They also had come in 2010 and 2011. Gene and Lila are dear friends who go back in time to the youth of our children. They helped the mural become a reality, so lovingly in so many ways. Gene, a retired electrical engineer with a ton of energy, found many tasks to improve life at the cemetery. He performed small electrical repairs, helped assess the wall structure, cleaned up tree limbs, but his most cherished asset to me was his moral support. Lila and I had a bond that was forged to new depths when we had traveled together to Romania with medical supplies along with spiritual first aid to the Romanians. She was not only a seasoned prayer warrior but her personality easily fit as a hostess to the many guests who entered the gates. Because our volunteer helpers had strict instructions to not allow the artist to be interrupted, she would divert them. She had many lively conversations with people as she diligently intercepted people who would casually begin to ask me questions or discuss the painting. There were times I allowed my concentration to be broken. But each day I would pray for the wisdom to know the difference between distractions and Divine appointments.

Gene and Lila were indispensable to the work. They were

hearty in faith and knew how to weather my storms, great and small. They were always quick to forgive if I crossed a line with my tone or attitude. These are the kind of folks you want around you in stress-filled times: people who know your heart and will not take a negative cranky mood too seriously. Lila was a master of redemptive distraction. Out of the blue she would start with "Remember the time...?" And we would take a trip down memory lane. These were memories of things our kids had done together or even testimonies of how God would send us out on Divine assignments, or a comical situation that made us all laugh.

God continued to stir the hearts of people to join the mural team. From September to November, eight people from the United States came for varying lengths of time to support the work through prayer and practical assistance. In addition to Gene and Lila, Bonnie, and Majel, my daughter-in-law Julie came with her friend Kelly. This was a great delight to me because other than Carl, she is the only one in my immediate family that has come to Israel.

When Julie called me to say she had booked her ticket and was so excited, I said, "That's great! *Where are you going?"* She really had not let on to me that she desired to come. If she had said something, apparently I did not recall it since as a registered nurse, she worked full time. It had not even entered my mind that she would be able to come! "I am coming to Israel. Kelly [Julie's close friend] is coming with me. We are going to be the best helpers you have ever had!" Shocked, I could barely believe my ears! Not only did they come to Israel, they were excellent assistants in the mural work.

Marlys was the last volunteer to come during the 2013 fall session. She was a Wisconsinite and had not been to Israel previously. Marlys and I were close in age and had plenty to talk about. It was fun to have her. She had no desire to go touring about. She was content to help me; that was enough for her. I was amazed by the love of God coming to me through people to strengthen me so I could continue with the mural painting.

CHAPTER 39

Stop Her!

Throughout the mural painting times, the spiritual warfare would intensify and then retreat in an unpredictable design. Not only was I learning to be swift with my offensive weapon, my sword of the Word, the Bible, but I knew how to ask for assistance from the believers around me. Additionally I knew all of the varied trials and pressures were helping transform me from one level of maturity to the next. This was my consolation during times when the opposition reached fevered pitch. It was the most intense tribulations that change me deep down where I could not change myself.

One such time occurred right after two sets of volunteers left and I was alone for 4 days until the next set arrived. One night as I lay sleeping, I heard, or felt, something that woke me up. I heard a loud noise like a bang or pop that woke me with a start! I felt someone in the room. I recognized the presence of a spirit of some kind. I took authority over it and commanded it to leave immediately in the name of Jesus. I lay back down and went to sleep. When I woke up, I noticed an unwelcome pressure in my head on the right side of my forehead. It was not acute but it was a familiar *'messenger from the devil'* kind of headache. I have had many headaches in my day, including migraines, but this headache comes with a standard set of symptoms all its own. Because of my redemption through the blood of Jesus and my faith in His complete power over the darkness, curses cannot kill me, or do permanent damage. But the battle is real and there are times when it can be quite distressing. At my midafternoon break, I laid down on a wooden bench in the cemetery and did not feel like painting. I decided to go home and rest. I also prayed. Thankfully I slept through the night.

In the morning I was hoping all would be normal but the poking pain began to ramp up and, over the course of the day, the pain became excruciating. In my imagination I could almost see a piece of half-inch rebar steel being plunged into the corner of my forehead. Life had to stop at this point as the pain became unbearable. Again I went home but could not even lay down. I walked ever so slowly around the flat. I was barely moving but attempting to cope with the misery one moment at a time. I did manage to sleep but early in the wee hours the pain intensified and woke me up. *"Oh Lord! I can't take this! It is TOO MUCH! Oh God, you have got to take this from me. Strengthen me, Jesus."* With every breath I prayed again. The intensity of what clearly was an enemy onslaught attempted to defy my faith.

The morning light filtered softly into the apartment. In an effort to distract myself from the pain, I navigated slowly to the kitchen table and sat down. When I did I saw an open vision. It had motion and audio. I saw a swirling spiraling whirlwind of darkness. I will not give any more details of this experience but I sensed the Lord allowed me to see this for a reason. I saw Satan's fury and pure hatred toward the Son of God and his plan to re-double his efforts to turn the entire world against Yeshua/Jesus Christ. His plan has always been to diminish who Jesus is, attempting to convince people that He is an ordinary man—a good teacher, yes, and a prophet, too, but not the Son of God and certainly NOT God come in the flesh. Clearly this ugly vision was connected to the assault I was under. More groanings too deep for words came from my spirit. It felt like I was being tortured. *"Yeshua!"* Now I was calling out audibly for my Beloved who always rescues me from 'the hurtful sword' (Psalm 144:10).

At about two p.m., still suffering beyond my ability to deal with it, I went to my Bible and found Scriptures from the book of Micah leaping off the page into my weary heart.

> *Mic 5:9-12 Thine hand shall be lifted up upon thine adversaries, and all thine enemies shall be cut off.*
> *And it shall come to pass in that day, says the LORD, that I will cut off thy horses out of the midst of thee, and I will destroy thy chariots:*
> *And I will cut off the cities of thy land, and throw down all thy strong holds:*
> *And I will cut off witchcrafts out of thine hand; and thou shalt have no more soothsayers:*

These words gave me a solid message of hope. I grabbed these words like a drowning person grabbing a life preserver. Deliverance was on the horizon. The pain persisted but over the next hour it began to slightly diminish. Three hours later, the piercing subsided considerably. By nine p.m. the strike was over. Exhausted, I collapsed on my bed and slept until morning.

Although I was thankful that my head no longer hurt, my soul was ravaged by the strength of this onslaught. I began to pray in earnest for answers so that if there was something I could do to prevent future battles like this one, I would certainly do whatever was required. I continued to be mystified that the enemy had the power to carry out a sustained strike like this. Had I given ground to the enemy unknowingly? Was the fact that I was alone significant in this analysis? Why would someone curse me, a lowly painter in a graveyard? Could it be because the paintings reveal the One who is the Living Truth, Messiah of Israel? Could it be I was a target because the art cries and exposes the darkness? The mural holds out the Word of Life in picture form, the universal language and defies the rejection of Messiah by His own. The dark powers of the prince of the air have not disappeared since the time of Yeshua's crucifixion and resurrection. Though He disarmed them, they are still trying to kill His name and defame Him. *This is why the art must cry out the truth of God's Word on the stone walls!*

I needed to talk to Roger. I felt like I needed prayer to recover from this trial and hoped that he and Ellen could pray with me. When I called they agreed immediately to meet me. I poured out my heart about what had happened. Anger spilled over when I asked if somehow my name was out there in the public realm. Who was responsible? I really wanted to blame somebody, anybody. Roger's offering surprised me and silenced me as well. He said, "Yes, your name is out there. You have inspired many people by what you are doing. This is a good thing. Really, I do not think you can separate yourself from the mural. You may need to adapt and learn to withstand whatever may come against you, knowing that the Lord is with you and will see you through." This was not an answer I had hoped for, even though inwardly Roger's words gave me courage to keep painting. I am grateful that there was not another attack like this one then or since. By now my peace was restored. Over the next few days, as I prayerfully pondered this experience and read my Bible, I concluded that there will be times we must suffer for the sake of the gospel. It is not easy but it is our honor. Like the Apostle Paul, may we say:

Gal 6:17 *From henceforth let no man trouble me: for I bear in my body the marks of the Lord Jesus.*

As the world zooms closer to the end of this age, and evil has succeeded in 'dressing very nicely,' it strikes me that the devil has been busy doing exactly what the vision had illustrated so graphically. He is using social pressure to discredit Jesus Christ all around the world. Mind control is an even better descriptor for this diabolical strategy. It is my feeling now that the Lord permitted that attack and the vision so I would be an able watchman in the disquieting days to come. These are the days that will be filled with shakings of every kind. The book of Hebrews speaks of a promise from God that once more He will shake not only the earth but the heavens also until all that remains is UNSHAKEABLE. The reality of sin, the need for redemption, Messiah's mandate to become the Passover Lamb, and the ultimate plans for those who will become his own and for those who will refuse Him, are all unshakeable truths. These are the bedrock of a faith that will triumph in the end.

CHAPTER 40

Red Hot!

Red hot. These two words sum up the 2014 mural session in Jerusalem. Carl, Scott, Gene and Lila, and later Karen and Virginia, comprised the mural team and much activity took place including the varnishing of the first half of the mural.

It was so wonderful to have Carl with me once again. His road to recovery from cancer was about a year in length. But there he was. Sometimes I would mentally pinch myself to see if it was all real. He fit in there, like a hand in a glove! My best times were always when Carl was there and together we contended for the prize.

We began our stay at a small guesthouse, "The Apple of His Eye," that was managed by local believers who had become friends during the mural painting process. Simantov and Linda were a Jew and Gentile combo, respectively, and were also kindred hearts for the Gospel. Carl and I were there for a week before Gene and Lila arrived. We had some wonderful times of worship at the guesthouse.

The one drawback to staying at this otherwise nice place was the noise. It is located on the corner of two hectic streets. The deafening roar of big construction trucks that literally shook the earth, thunderous motorcycles and constant beep beep....HONKKKK, was too much for this artist. I needed quiet. I needed calm when I was resting and attempting to revive so I could keep painting. We decided to move to a different apartment on the edge of the city. Here the quiet was like music to my ears.

Our time at "The Apple of His Eye Guesthouse" was providential, however. This couple became dear to us. They stood with us in prayer time again and again. Later Simantov agreed to a photo shoot to model for my painting of Apostle Paul. When I used live models it was not to create a likeness of the person necessarily. Real faces and figures always initiated a successful mural scene because of realistic proportion and dimension. But when I painted Apostle Paul, he looked very much like my model. Simantov did not seem to mind too much and we all had fun with his cameo appearance on the rear mural wall.

With Carl, Scott, Gene and Lila on duty for the first half of this season, we prepared the mural for its first coat of sealant with repairs, cleaning and touch-ups. Gene had done the research and found the correct product that we needed and had it shipped last fall. The men who would apply the sealant were provided without charge by the Israeli company who sold us the product. The sealant is not only protecting the mural, it is helping show off the color and detail work too! The mural looked fresh and brighter than ever. Additional sealant would be applied to the second part of the mural as well as a second coat about a year after the mural was completed. It really felt good to get this process started. We all wanted the mural to last indefinitely.

Leaving the varnishing of the mural in the competent hands of Gene Anderson, Carl and I took a holiday from work to drive up to the Golan Heights. The north of Israel is the most beautiful landscape I have ever laid eyes on. It was so refreshing to leave the hectic, noisy city life of Jerusalem and to sail up the panoramic Jordan Valley to the mountainous region of northern Israel. We drove to some special places with more incredible vistas of the Hula Valley, the Naphtali Mountains and the gorgeous and stately Mount Hermon. The summit still had traces of snow on its slopes. The raw beauty of this soft lavender and multiple peaked range against the cerulean expanse of the cloudless sky took my breath away.

There was something here, much deeper, that was not to be viewed with the eyes, but grasped with the inner soul. The passionate love that God has for this land and the people of this land is the rationale for planting his own tried and true warrior children in this glorious place. We met some of these believers and had the privilege of sharing times of worship with them.

One of the people we met was a woman named Mariam who lived in a village down the slopes of the Golan Heights. She was very soft spoken with a distinct twinkle in her eye. It was not easy to tell if this was a tear in disguise or if it was a sparkle of inner joy. Now that I know her better, I can say with assurance, it is both. Mariam is a lady of Jewish Polish descent and is the daughter of a Holocaust survivor. She told me her story in detail about losing two hundred family members to the Holocaust. There were only four relatives left alive. The unthinkable tragedy experienced by so many Jewish people at the hands of Hitler staggers the imagination. Yet here she is living in the land of her forefathers, regathered after thousands of years of dispersion. I immediately loved this gal. Maybe, just maybe, the fact that she is an accomplished artist might be a part of what drew me to her.

Getting to know Mariam and visiting her village was a real treat for us. It amazed us to realize that she was a 'planting of the Lord' in an area of Israel where there were few who believed. I saw that Mariam's life was like a flaming torch against the night sky. She did not need to shout or cry out about her faith. She just lived it every day.

Carl left for home shortly after our appointment in the north. Gene and Lila also left for the states about ten days later. As usual, when Carl left, I was a little melancholy. Each time we had to separate, we called upon the Lord for that gift of grace to be apart. Our marriage has only been strengthened by these times. It has become obvious to both of us that during these times, the Lord does a special inner work of trust-building and enduring love that he lovingly embroiders on the inside of each of us.

My consolation was the two new helpers arriving in a few days. Virginia, from Wisconsin, was a more recent friend who was experienced in prayer and intercession and my friend from church, and my pastor's wife, Karen. They were a super duo. Virginia kept the worship flames fanned along with Scott and his trusty guitar, while Karen applied her art skills to help quicken my progress. I soon discovered a part of her I had not previously been acquainted with—her ability to focus! Nothing could distract Karen. She painted everything I asked her to. She even painted the drapery (art term for clothing) on some of the figures, which is something I dislike to paint. Karen is an artist in her own right and possesses an advanced level of art ability, which I was happy to utilize. Karen had not been to Israel before and soon found that her ability to concentrate on her task helped her navigate the choppy waters of life in Jerusalem.

During this session, I had a special visitor join us from the north of Israel. I really love how our lives are so beautifully entwined at key moments for God's kingdom purposes. Mariam, from the north, came to Jerusalem. I had no idea how our lives would touch one another's when we first met. But the Lord had quite an amazing plan. He had his eye on the mural in Jerusalem and the mural painter and wanted to touch Mariam, His beloved artist who had endured so much.

When Mariam made the trip down to visit me, she had not painted for years. Time and pressure of all sorts had caused her to lay her brush down. I respected her decision and wanted to be sensitive. However, it seemed to me that the absence of her artistic outlet was sorrowful for her. I longed to put a paintbrush in her hand and ask for help with the mural. I asked the Lord, "Is it time for Mariam to paint again?"

Mariam was encouraging to me in the mural work. She expressed her approval of the mural art that was finished so far. This was meaningful to me and strengthened me. As I mixed paint for the first background layer that eventually would be the book of Acts, I decided to risk asking for Mariam's help. To my delight, Mariam said, "Okay," and without missing a stride, put on an old shirt I offered her and a hat to shield her eyes from the brilliant sun, took the brush and the paint and quickly covered the assigned area. I then took her a little farther in her painting renewal and asked for some real artwork on the scene of the ascension. I already knew her skill with figures and asked her to paint the people who watched our Messiah disappear into the clouds above. I left her alone and the Lord met her. Mariam painted, Jesus set her free to flow in her artistic gifts once again. When I came back to give her some feedback about how much I liked the figures she painted, she said something that revealed the depth of her brokenness. *"I can't believe that you would even allow me to touch this mural. You will never know how the Lord has used this time to help me to be able to use my gift of art once again."* I was overjoyed and moved to tears at the same time. We have become friends since this time. We have spent time painting together up in the beautiful north country, bonded forever with a love so far beyond what we can think or imagine: a love that heals, a love that lifts.

CHAPTER 41

Secrets of the Mural

One brilliant sunny morning, Meir came to the foot of the scaffold. "Patricia, there is a teacher coming to visit today. He is bringing his class, too." I took a deep breath as I straightened up on the scaffold platform. "Great!" was my response as I twisted to stretch out a few muscle kinks. Shortly after noon, a man entered along with about 20 eleven- to thirteen-year-old young people. I heard him speaking in Hebrew to his group and pointing to the images of Creation on the mural. I continued to paint but inwardly I was very happy to see the mural being used this way. Meir and I had agreed in advance that I would not give a tour. We did not want to do or say anything that could even come close to the appearance of proselytizing the youth as it is illegal in Israel.

As I continued to paint the scenes of King David and the Ark of the Covenant, I became aware of quietness. I quickly look down the wall to behold the children all sitting down on the edge of the stone walkway with their Bibles opened on their laps. They were each silently reading the biblical stories that were illustrated before their eyes. The teacher then called the children to follow him and they approached the scaffold. "May the children ask you a few questions? I will translate into English." "Yes, of course."

The questions were the normal questions I was frequently asked: what kind of paint, did you sketch out the entire mural first, how did you choose each scene, etc. But then the children asked for something I had never heard expressed before. *"Can we have your autograph?"* I laughed out loud. "I am not famous, you know, maybe a little bit here, but not in America." This did not deter their zeal to receive my signature in their notebooks. As I complied, I heard myself announce that if they would return and bring their parents with them, that I would reveal the secrets of the mural to them. They left the cemetery then. Meir and I rejoiced in this happy time.

One afternoon the following week, a woman came in with two older children and a very young child in tow. I had not noticed at first. But soon Meir came to tell me that these were two of the children who had visited with the class and that they had brought their mother in to see the mural. Instantly I recalled my invitation to bring the parents so I scooted down from the scaffold to the ground and approached and then greeted them. The children's mother was a dear woman who was open and friendly. She said she would like to hear about those secrets I promised to reveal. I sensed a God appointment was taking place. Starting with Creation and then Adam and Eve, I began to tell my little group about the fruit of the tree of the knowledge of good and evil. I pointed out that the fruit that was in the sunshine looked enticing to Eve and so she was tempted. But in the shadow side of the tree the fruit resembled shriveled-up human brains, which depicted the true nature of the forbidden fruit. I reported that this was one secret of the mural. The tree of the knowledge of good and evil was revealing a powerful truth of how its consumption would exploit the minds of people and take them from God.

Next I asked my inquisitors if they knew who the lion

was and why he was standing on the snake? We had a lively discussion about God's secret plan to help us all come back to Him through the Messiah, who the prophets foretold would be from the tribe of Judah as represented by the lion. He would destroy all of the evil that was represented by the snake called Satan. The children's mother spoke English well and translated everything I said to the others. On we walked and talked about the mural pictures. Even when the youngest became restless and whiny, the others were undeterred. I asked the woman if they wanted me to continue as we came to the end of the Tenach and the beginning of the New Covenant. As the woman encouraged me to continue my presentation, I spoke deep truths about the virgin birth of Jesus, His miracles, claims, then His fulfillment as the Lamb who takes away the sins of the world. When we stood in front of the lamb ascending the hill of Calvary, I spoke of the forgiveness I had received from God and how this in turn empowered me to love others in a new way. Tears flowed as they often do when I speak about the miracle of redemption that I had experienced. The woman began to weep also. I opened my arms and she fell into my embrace and continued to cry. Something was happening and it was marvelous. Our tears turned to laughter when we continued to walk and talk. She said, "I have been depressed lately—too many worries. When the children told me of their visit here in the cemetery and about the promise of the mural secrets, I thought to myself, maybe I should hear this. This may be what I need."

There were many amazing exchanges that took place as I painted the mural each spring and fall. One day when I was on the big ladder painting the prophets, a Jewish foursome, two couples, came in and began to view the mural. The New Covenant was already on the wall. I had returned to this section to complete it before I resumed the coverage of the back wall. As they neared the end of the Tanakh and the beginning of the New Covenant, I saw them hesitate and because they were in earshot, I could hear their conversation, which was in English. They said, "Let's go back now." I invaded their conversation and said in a sweet voice, "And that is OK! You may look at as much or as little as you want. We want you to be blessed." They seemed surprised that I, the artist, was speaking to them. They immediately came up to my ladder and began to express their appreciation of the mural and its images. They began to ask me all kinds of questions like, "Why are you doing this? Is this a commission, and are you getting paid? Aren't you fearful to be here with so much going on in the streets?" I came down the ladder and stood with them. I answered one question at a time. Then one of the women wrapped her arms around me and thanked me for all I had done. I was surprised at this demonstration of affection and acceptance, but it touched me deeply.

Another memorable interaction was a tour I conducted with four teachers who came from Tel Aviv. As I presented various scenes of the mural, I would insert some of the secrets that people so enjoyed hearing about. These four were loud and lively. They had a day off from their teaching jobs and were having a good time. They were quizzing one another about some of the less common scenes and then laughing at one another's responses when they got it wrong. When we came to the beginning of the New Covenant, I said, "You are Jewish and I respect you. This tour is finished now. If you want me to continue, I will only go on if you ask me to do so." They thought only for one second and then one man said, "It is okay. You don't have to worry about us, please continue." I looked at the others who each nodded vigorously. So I began to talk about the prophecies and the virgin birth of Jesus and that He was no ordinary man. On I went, talking about the ministry of Jesus and why He came. Now it was my turn to laugh, although I did it inwardly. This raucous group, who had been so animated, became increasingly quiet. In fact, they became quite sober as though contemplating every word I spoke. When we reached the end of the mural, they offered sincere thanks and out they went. The impact of the message of the mural on this group was tangible. I would have loved to have been a fly on the wall to hear the inevitable discussion that surely followed.

Every fall there is a city wide happening in Jerusalem called "Inside Out." It is a two-day event when all the historic buildings and locations are open and free to the public. The Alliance International Cemetery is on the map as well. Because of the interesting people buried there it is considered an historic tourist attraction. If the weather is nice, it is not unusual for over a thousand people to enter the gates during the two days, in large and small groups, to have official tours. Meir provides a lively and interesting tour of the stories. When he gets near the wall, he calls for me to come and assist by presenting the story of the mural to the groups. These visitors are Israelis but most can understand English to some degree. Together we have a fun time. Their response to us is always positive. I have had two women at different times come and grab my arm and tell me that they can feel "love in this place." There are times I will include in my presentation the story of my deliverance from the occult and my love for God. People listen eagerly but rather than speak publically, they will come to me privately and want to tell me that they could relate to my story, or sometimes they want to know more about my faith. Some will return at a later date and begin to express an interest more freely than with a group of their contemporaries.

During one "Inside Out" event, Meir and I were at the back wall, explaining to the group about the Lamb and the

Good News. The presence of the Lord was tangible. There seemed to be a holy hush over the group. A man said to me, "I have never heard this." Many Jewish people have heard some facsimile of the Gospel and dismissed it. Yet I would venture to say that most Jews have never heard the *true* Gospel message. If and when they do, it gives them pause. I believe it is a pause that causes them to think for themselves about the message and the messenger.

One young Jewish man began to visit the cemetery on a regular basis. Benyamin (not his real name) would walk down to the end or maybe just halfway and sit quietly, sometimes for an hour or more. When he expressed an interest in not only the message of the mural, but also in us, we began to have an interesting dialogue with him. He voiced many thoughts and concerns about the Gospel and about the Torah and the Rabbis' teachings. Benyamin began reading the New Covenant. One by one, starting with Meir, we all spent time with him. We would answer questions and attempt to encourage him to keep seeking the Lord, seeking the truth.

The day came when Benyamin announced that he had studied the Scriptures thoroughly and prayed diligently and came to the conclusion that Yeshua is the Jewish Messiah. When he spoke these words, it initiated a presence of the Holy Spirit that impacted him in a wondrous way. This expression of faith triggered a rebirth and transformation journey that changed his life. He has become not only a good friend but a brother in the faith as well. He told me later that he needed every scene on the mural to understand who Yeshua is and what the Gospel message is really all about.

There have been and continue to be many amazing encounters with the people who come in to visit the cemetery. As we approach our visitors with open hearts and a friendly smile, a bridge begins to be built. It is a bridge of love and understanding that helps people feel at home with us. It gives them confidence about who we are and conveys the message that they are valued by us.

These are the very experiences that kept me returning to complete the mural. I was thrilled to think that God was touching the lives of the people who entered the gates.

CHAPTER 42

Bogged Down but Not For Long

The fall of 2014 brought considerable progress to the mural painting. Prayer volunteers Dolean, Deloris, Dayle, and then Sally joined me at various points throughout the season. Lois from Portugal was a volunteer whose surprise help came when I needed it most. Scott of course was present throughout the session. I had learned how to pace myself so things flowed fairly evenly for a while. I was bouncing back and forth from the details of the final scenes on the long side wall and the newer scenes after Jesus' resurrection.

Things began to bog down, however, when the workers came in to build a short roof over the mural. This was necessary protection from the elements. The workers were men from the Mount of Olives who were Muslim. They spoke almost no English except for the boss. He spoke a little English. They were all very respectful of us as we did our job and they did theirs. We would have occasional lighthearted interactions and sometimes share food items for lunch. Several times I attempted to explain the Gospel using the mural scenes. (We felt our best witness is love and respect to them as well.) There was a problem, however. It was not the men but what came in with them—*the spirit of Islam.* Shortly after these men came into the cemetery, I literally could not paint. The paint on my palette felt like mud as I pushed it around with my brush. My brain felt scrambled. It was so very frustrating I wanted to scream. There was an invisible force oppressing my mind and my creative abilities. Of course, at first, I blamed the sudden resistance to painting on the weather, my mood, not enough sleep, etc., until I felt the Holy Spirit opened my eyes to see the truth. Especially when the men were in close proximity, everything seemed to slow down to a crawl. The paint would literally not flow off my brush. When I realized that once again the spiritual battle had ramped up, I grabbed Scott and said, "Let's worship the Lord for a while." There were times when we had to press in to prayer and worship for over an hour before the resistance would be overpowered by the Holy Spirit in us.

One difficult day when the workers were present, I was painting the Pentecost scene. In my opinion, this is one of the most significant scenes on the mural. I was stuck. After more prayer, I heard the Holy Spirit say, *"Go up on the scaffold and paint there for now. Come back to this later when you do not have to fight this spirit."* As I clambered onto the scaffold to paint the scene of Jesus feeding the 5,000, I had a lot more freedom to accomplish my goal for the day. Spiritual warfare is an interesting phenomenon. It does not follow logic nor reason. But our spiritual weapons must be clearly directed by the One who is the head over all principality and powers of the air—*the One* who has triumphed over them openly. Once I understand the nature of the opposition, I can function again—I know what to do. Then it is just a matter of persistence and time before relief comes on the scene.

The crew boss was quite impressed with us and the task at hand. He seemed genuinely interested in the mural and expressed that He thought it was beautiful. He always tried to be helpful to me. He decided to build a set of steps for the scaffold. I think he recognized that using the ladder was a bit shaky for me, especially since I tended to be going up and down frequently. I was quite happy to have the steps. He clearly enjoyed my gratitude when the steps where finished and he saw me happily using them every day.

Not all of our new friends brought a battle with them. One of the amazing provisions of the Lord that helped us break through the times of oppression were the new friends who would come into the cemetery at key moments. One of these new friends was an Israeli woman who was a believer and a dancer. She would come on holidays and release the Holy Spirit through her dance ministry. She had the ability to gather others into her dances and together they would bring down heaven right in the middle of the cemetery. The local believers, who I have come to know and love, have remained friends and advocates. They are not new to the warfare, as they have also had to battle the unseen resistance in the same way I have.

CHAPTER 43

Race to the Finish Line

As the mural with its colorful images grew longer and approached the end of the back wall, I was energized to keep going. Spring and fall, spring and fall, I would come to paint. By the spring of 2015, the finished mural was looming ahead and the thrill was enough to revive a tired soul. The times at home were filled with bookkeeping and fulfilling the requirements for the small nonprofit organization Carl and I had started to help us achieve the goal. I also committed to speaking engagements at various churches and/or groups, prayer groups and, of course, precious time with my family. By this time I had four darling grandchildren: Serena, Grace, Jake, and David. It was hard to leave them so often and for so long. Yet I knew that as I was faithful to the call of God, the Lord would be faithful to bless and keep all of my family in the palm of His hand.

Back in Jerusalem, the following spring painting session was a season of extremes. Physically, I felt like I had experienced every condition imaginable: cold, rain, wind. Then, just as suddenly, the sun would shine its golden rays and the temperature would rise to hot and hotter. The changing conditions made it challenging to paint but with the help of the team, I adapted. There were days only a little painting could be done, but there were other days when I covered an amazing amount of wall with God's art!

Carl, Scott, Meir and I were the team for this session. We would settle down for a worship time each morning, discuss Bible scriptures, as well as communicate about various issues that had arisen. Our worship times were the hub and strength of the team. As Nehemiah states: it is necessary to have a trowel (paintbrush) in one hand and a sword in the other hand (a song in my mouth). We clearly averted attacks of the enemy attempting to penetrate our unity with strife and division. Jerusalem is like a pressure cooker. We really had to encourage and care for one another.

The fall session of 2015 was one of the most challenging of them all. I had anticipated that I would finish the mural during this session. Yet we did not have extra prayer volunteers this time. Thankfully Scott was present and, of course, Meir. We continued to worship in song and prayed often but it seemed as though the powers of darkness were pulling out all the stops for one last effort to sabotage "The Jerusalem Wall of Life Mural."

During that final session, we were subjected to a well-planned strategy by the enemy. It came in like a flood and tried to bring strife into our midst that could destroy our friendships and partnerships. By this time, I was worn out. It was difficult for me to cope with conflict, so I asked the Alliance Field Office for a mediator to sit with those of us who were involved. This is exactly what we needed to help sort out what was real and what were distortions sent by the enemy to undermine our unity. One of our Alliance partners, Pastor Joe, sat down with us. Together we prayed for resolution. As we surrendered our hearts and wills to God, grace came down from heaven. The love and respect that we held for one another came to the forefront and obliterated all of our objections and arguments. It is such an incredible resource to have people available who do not shy away from problems. When Scot Dressler became the new field director, he would say, "How well do we gain from the conflicts *when* they occur, not *'if'* they occur?" Both Scot and Joe has become skilled in the conflict resolution process as they guide many within the ranks, out of contention into agreement. Early on in the painting of the mural, when I was unseasoned and naïve, I complained to the Lord about a certain individual who was resisting me and causing some problems. The Holy Spirit reminded me of a verse in the Book of Proverbs in the Bible: (my paraphrase) "Where there are no oxen in the stall, it remains clean, but when there are oxen who are working to bring profits, there will be a needed mess in that stall," Proverbs 14:4. In my heart, I heard the instruction of the Holy Spirit: if I thought that I could do something for God but that there were no problems along the way, I may as well quit immediately. *"But when you are increasing My kingdom on earth it will get messy along the way; do not allow it to throw you off course or be offended."*

Is it any wonder that the final days of mural painting would take place in the midst of fiery trials and tribulation? Amidst the crescendo of pressure, there was one very bright spot. On one sunny warm day of the last week of painting, I was working on the final scenes when a woman came walking down the long stone pathway toward me. She was a welcome sight to me. As I began to greet her, she said, "I have something for you." She handed me a full bouquet of glowing yellow roses that took my breath away. "These are not from me. They truly are from the Lord… for you. When I woke up this morning I heard Him say to go and purchase yellow roses and to take them to Patricia." The words she spoke touched me deeply and I began to weep. She smiled sweetly, turned, and walked back on the stone pathway. Somehow she knew that I needed to be alone as

I digested this heavenly moment and this special gift. The recent pain and difficulties seemed to come to the surface all at once as I realized that truly my Heavenly Abba sent this gift to me. Although not audible, I heard *"Thank you Daughter"* in my spirit. He was recognizing all that it took to be obedient to the heavenly vision of creating a mural that tells His story.

The messenger of my glorious bouquet was none other than Esther Korson, formerly Esther Dorflinger. Esther is a Jewish/Israeli believer who is the author of a well-known book "I Am My Beloved's" that has reached tens of thousands of people around the world. She has become a dear friend. She has seen me at some of my worst times and would always have the right words to encourage me. True friends are forged in the fire. Esther has experienced many fiery times in her own life and among her many travels around the world with the message of Yeshua. She knew my work was born of God.

When Esther walked away my tears released. I felt the presence of the Lord in a unique way that is difficult to describe. It is like laughing and crying simultaneously. As I choked on a sob that welled up from the deep, I felt a joy that made me want to leap into the air like a gazelle. I was so happy to be finished with the mural I could hardly contain myself. After six and a half years of a formidable journey, an arduous climb, I was so close to the last brush stroke. I continued to bask in the moment of sublime victory. I believe the intense joy I felt was God's own joy. This was something He could use to reach out to people who may never entertain the Good News in any other venue. This mural was a tool that He has used and will continue to use to bring in those He longs for.

As the final stroke was in my sights, I badgered the Lord in prayer. "Is there anything else you want me to paint before

I stop and say, 'It is finished!'?" There were many spots I could change or improve upon, but I wanted to know His leading. This was His mural, His miracle, His story. There was one picture that remained in my heart and yet I felt I had to be certain it was from the Lord to paint. I had been considering it for over a year. It was the scene of the Mercy Seat on top of the Ark of the Covenant—the place where the sacrificial blood was applied by the high priest.

When the Lord gave Moses the ten commandments and then all the designs for the tabernacle and the ark of the covenant, He gave them as examples of something precious that already exists in the heavenly realm. These items contain unimaginable and holy information about the living God. In the book of Hebrews, in the New Covenant, we are taught that the Temple services and items were patterns of things in the heavens. They were copies of what was really in heaven and what would come when the Messiah gave Himself to be the sacrifice for sin. When the high priest sprinkled the mercy seat in the Holy of Holies, this act foretold the coming of the Son of God who would shed his blood and then applied his own blood there forevermore. Such a mystery baffles the sterile intellect that we seem to possess in these modern times.

Why did Jesus have to shed His blood to redeem us from the curse of this fallen world? Could He not have done the same thing in some other less painful, more fashionable way? The reason that this answer is an unequivocal "No!" is that, like the immutable laws that govern our world such as gravity and other laws of physics, heaven has immutable realities that we know not of—at least not yet! One of these laws is revealed, however, in both covenants in the Bible. This is that without the shedding of blood there is no remission of sin. The Lord said to Moses, *"The Life is the blood. The blood makes atonement for sin by the life,"* Leviticus 17:10.

When Yeshua intentionally went to the cross to die, He knew that by nature of being all God and all man, His blood alone served to qualify to do this work of remission—the ultimate and eternal payment for sin. God is love; He is also holy. Sin cannot be in His presence. This is why when we believe and receive Jesus and the sacrificial work on the cross by faith, we can now be in the presence of a Holy God and have a relationship with Him. I knew none of this when I faced my darkest hour and cried out a simple prayer to Jesus. I was not even sure, at that point in my life, that He really existed. I only knew my own pain and desperation. My cry brought God on a dead run to help me. This is an example of His passionate love for us. This love for us is what enabled Him to send His Son in the form of a human being to resolve this sin problem that came into the world through Adam and Eve. When I had hit 'rock bottom' in my younger days, my cry for help was actually an act of faith. I wanted to die but somewhere inside I still had a morsel of hope that there was something more. If I was convinced there was nothing after death, or deceived into thinking that dying would bring me relief from my woes, then I would have committed suicide. The idea had been growing in me for months. My whole being cried out in a silent scream for help from a good God. The Bible became my life coach. The application of the knowledge contained in it brought a powerful healing and a makeover to every facet of my life. Eventually I studied the finer details of God's plan for the redemption of all people, which is foretold through the first covenant and the Law of Moses all the way to the coming of Jesus to perform the ultimate.

To me, the mercy seat atop the Ark of the Covenant is a visual testimony of this ultimate plan of redemption and, in effect, created a new universe when Jesus completed the shedding of His blood and applied it in the heavens. This act not only provided forgiveness of sins but sealed the judgment against the devil and all of the powers of darkness, stripping them of their power over us who believe. The magnitude of the meaning of the blood on the mercy seat is so powerful that I don't think we have fully grasped it yet, but we will.

As I was finishing the scenes at the end of the back mural wall, the sense to paint the mercy seat was growing and taking on a certainty in my spirit. I continued to pray and the "YES!" continued to strengthen. I considered asking certain people whose opinions I respected whether they thought it would be good to include it. This had gotten me into trouble in the past, however. People can have all kinds of opinions but the opinion that matters is the Lord's. I decided to paint it because by this time I was sure the Lord was leading me to do so.

It was already in my mind to paint this scene in the sky realm in between the hill of Calvary and the resurrection scene. I painted the wings of the cherubim over the top of the ark, which was peeking out from the temple curtain, which was torn from top to bottom. This happened at the moment of Yeshua's death to signify that through his atoning blood, we now had access into the Holy of Holies—the very presence of God. I painted the colors of blue, purple, and scarlet on the torn curtain, finishing the scene with a pool of blood on top, where the mercy seat is, between the wings of the cherubim. I portrayed the blood running down just a little so it could be identified as blood. My final strokes of paint placed two lines forming a small cross over the blood on the mercy seat. The cross was very small, barely noticeable from the sidewalk view. Again, I sensed a witness and a whisper in my spirit that the presence of this cross shape would leave no doubt in anyone's mind that this is not '*another Jesus*' as Paul warned about. It is not '*another Jesus*' who is touted among New Agers who are in deep deception. It was not some other gospel with a Jesus who did not go to the cross as a substitute for sin for us, but this is the One and only Yeshua, Jesus, the anointed one from God, sent to perform this incredible act of redemption for all who would receive Him. *I could almost feel all hell trembling at the sight of the last scene God gave me to paint.*

Standing back to survey the vignette, I was stilled by the holiness of what I had painted. As I stood quietly, worship came forth from my spirit to my Savior, and I thought about this most incredible love story of all time. A gentle and soft voice spoke in my spirit, *"Even many of my own do not yet fully understand the depths of this scene."*

Slowly I came back to the present. A new reality hit my entire being like a bolt of lightning! It is finished! It is finished! The mural is finished!!

Your Mural Gallery

Race to the Finish Line

CHAPTER 44

Backlash

The level of oppression and pressure those last few weeks was one of the most severe I had ever experienced. I was exhausted to the point of collapse. The popular poem about the two sets of footprints along the beach representing the Lord walking alongside his child illustrated me after the mural was finished, but truly the footprints turned into a single set and the Lord was carrying me. He was certainly carrying me through those next several weeks. I was in bed for three days. The oppression and exhaustion combined began to produce anxiety in my body. For anyone who has never experienced anxiety or panic attacks, consider yourself very blessed. I would rather have physical pain than anxiety. It is so unsettling with feelings like everything is going to spin out of control. It actually is a form of low level pain, in my opinion. I began to wonder if I was about to have a breakdown. The mere thought of this sent anxiety and panic throughout my being. I called to God with the desperation that was building up within me.

On the third morning after the mural was finished, I woke up with increased anxiety and panic. *Oh no!* This is it, fearing a breakdown was taking place. Suddenly I leapt out of bed. I began praying out loud in my heavenly prayer language and walked rapidly throughout my flat. I took authority over every spirit that was oppressing my body, my mind, and my emotions. I resisted them audibly in the name of Yeshua, supreme King over all principalities and powers. "Sing! I need to sing and worship the Lord," my inner thoughts directed me now in a clear fashion. I went to my autoharp and grabbed the chords to a favorite warfare song.

You, O Lord, are my fortress,
My Deliverer, and my strength.
You, my God, are my High Tower,
You avenge me of my enemies.
I will trust in you and I will not be afraid.
Yes, I will trust in you and I will not be afraid.
Though storms may come and darkness may surround me;
I need not fear for You become my light.
I abide in the tabernacle of the Most High
Yes, I dwell in the safety of His love.
Written by Bonita Van Domelen

At that point, I needed this song. I sang with all of my heart. I sang it repeatedly, at least 15 times. As I have heard it said, desperate times call for extreme measures. By the tenth time through this song, the fear began to leave and so did the anxiety. After an hour *all* of the breakdown symptoms had disappeared. The anxiety was gone, the panic and fear were replaced with an increasing sense of peace. The only persisting problem was a sense of deep fatigue in my body. I realized this would take a little time and rest to get over.

Successfully coming through this battle built up my faith about the reality of the operations of dark powers and our ability to overcome them through Jesus. It is not easy to learn this lesson. If they can convince us that all of our experience is natural, then we respond in the natural. The reality was I was not having a breakdown, but the enemy took advantage of my weakened state to bring strong sensations that sure made it feel like I was on the edge.

Had I not known about the reality of spiritual forces that could oppress us, I would have entertained the possibility of medical help. But now I was on higher ground and so very thankful to the Lord for getting me through this trying time. I know believers who have had breakdowns, and this can happen despite our best efforts and prayer power. Many factors go into a vulnerable state like this. No two are the same. But our faithful God will bring us through no matter what condition we may find ourselves in.

As part of my rest and recovery I was planning to visit the Island of Cyprus to see some new friends who lived there. I had never been to Cyprus and was looking forward to being there. There was one nagging problem. I had caught a cold that quickly turned into an upper respiratory infection. I am sure my immune system was on overload from all the stress. The fatigue did not help matters. My friends there received me with joy, despite the nasty bug I brought with me. They cared for me and prayed for me. I went about the island with them and was able to see some of the beauty there.

When I flew back to Ben Gurion Airport, I picked up my car from the long term parking lot. Because of the dense traffic, I drove at a literal crawl on Highway 1 up to Jerusalem. As I drove, the presence of a deep peace came over me and I felt the honor of God to be back in this place.

CHAPTER 45

The Challenge of Jerusalem

The apartment that we rented in Arnona was near the famous overlook of Jerusalem called the Haas Promenade. Despite being a country girl, living in the city on the fourth floor of a large complex worked quite well for me; of course, this was not just any city. To say Jerusalem is special is a criminal understatement. It is a beautiful city in so many respects. Oh, it has a few negative features like crazy traffic and high prices, but the good and precious points outweigh the negative by far. On the physical level it is a city of contrasts. I love the old white stone buildings that date back anywhere from 100 to 1,000 years. These walls of Jerusalem stone, especially those in the Old City, give me a feeling of refuge in a howling storm. Maybe it is the tumultuous history they represent but *I feel God.* Even if I was not a Christian, I think I would get a sense of God's existence just from being in the presence of those hallmarks of time. It gives that sense of the ancient in the present. A glimpse of the Old City walls as I drive about still takes my breath away. Yet, right next door is the new Mamilla Mall, with ultra-modern and trendy stores and restaurants. As I walk about the city it is common to be caressed with the fragrance of Bougainvilla and other sweet smelling botanicals, only to be blasted in the face for a brief moment with a smell of rotten garbage or worse, urine. Contrasts of all kinds abound in Jerusalem. I have learned to love them—most of them, but especially the contrasts in the people who live there as well as those who visit.

From my very first visit in 1998 when I described earlier how in the midst of thousands of Orthodox Jews I heard the loving voice of my Heavenly Father say, "No one can take your place in my heart," I have had a deep God-given love for the Orthodox and Ultra-Orthodox Jews. When I learned about their fervency for God in all things, and how their daily lives revolve around the Scriptures, I was awakened to what the Apostle Paul wrote in the book of Romans, chapter 10, that the Jews have a zeal for God but not according to knowledge. They continue in the first covenant, not considering that the awaited Messiah came and went and will return again. Paul also writes that they are blind in part—notice it says *in part,* therefore not totally. They love God, the God of their patriarchs, Abraham, Isaac and Jacob, and Moses. I walk among them in Jerusalem in silence with a constant prayer in my heart for them to come to see fully who this merciful, amazing God is and the incredible plan of redemption that is theirs. Oh that they could understand the amazing grace that is available to them. I love them because the Lord loves them and will fulfill His plan for Israel's salvation in His time.

Living in this unique metropolis is a feat in itself. I have heard it said more than once, "You don't choose Jerusalem, Jerusalem chooses you." I have heard others say, even Israelis, that life in Jerusalem is like living in a pressure cooker and they cannot live here. I say you must have the grace from God Himself to live here and flourish. People of all ethnicities, both Jewish and non-Jewish, live throughout Israel, but especially here in Jerusalem. The diversity is abundant. I can stand on a crowded street corner downtown and in the crowd hear three or four languages being spoken at once. Contrasts abound; it is an honor and a blessing to be here but a difficult challenge at the same time.

For me, having our first long term rental contract was a milestone in faith in this entire journey of living in Jerusalem. Trusting the Lord to provide for this place of lodging took some time to arrive at. It is one thing to step out in faith, but quite another to stay strong in that faith when the funds run low and the rent is coming due. It is referred to as 'stretching' in the world of Christian vernacular. I was stretched several times through the painting campaign but every time, without fail, the provision would come through before I was in financial trouble. I finally began to relax in the whole issue of finances and trust him with confidence and calm.

Knowing it would be advantageous to have a renter for this apartment when I left for a few months, I placed an ad in the local believer's newsletter, praying my way through each decision—even how to construct the ad to get the kind of person that would take responsibility for my place and keep it nice. But the people who would rent from me came from a different direction entirely. Friends from the US who were in the process of applying for citizenship were interested in renting the flat. I was overjoyed! Daniel and Elizabeth were relatively new friends of mine but had quickly advanced to dear friends in the last couple of years. They lived in the north woods for a few years and our respective fellowship groups became acquainted with one another. Because of our mutual Israel connection we knew we had to meet. It was fun to be in on the first segment of their journey to Jerusalem. They have since been busy living their own amazing story of how the Lord brought them to Israel. To have them stay at our apartment was such a comfort to me. Leaving it in good hands, I soon embarked on my flight back to Spooner, Wisconsin.

CHAPTER 46

A Beautiful Hot Day

Throughout the years of mural painting, the topic of a mural dedication ceremony had been discussed. The first person to have a vision for a dedication event was Roger, former director of the Alliance. Although he was retired by that time, he continued to support the idea. This would be a time for all who had a part in this massive undertaking to come together, and prayerfully commit this work into the hands of God. It would be a time of celebration!

I insisted that Roger be a big part of it and planning it, as well as participating in the actual program itself. It also just so happened to be the anniversary of the Alliance Church in the land of Israel, celebrating 75 years. The Alliance was already planning a celebration event and thought it would work well to place the mural dedication in this sequence of events in May of 2016.

By the time I finished the mural, Marshall was field director. His wife, Babs, was also very active in the day-to-day operations of the Alliance Church. These two were a great combination. Marshall was a rock and vivacious Babs was the creative thinker. I feel very close to them. Like Roger, they had to come to my rescue more than once during times of extreme pressure, to pray with me and encourage me.

Babs and I were the primary planners for the dedication. Babs is a skilled graphic designer and led in the preparation of invitations and flyers. The time came quickly. It seemed like I had no sooner landed back in Spooner in mid-January when I had to reserve flights for Carl and I to return to Jerusalem for the dedication event. I really had not fully rested up from the previous trip, when Carl and I were winging our way over the Atlantic once again.

We settled into our familiar place quickly and began to engage in the numerous and varied activities that included making brochures, cleaning up the cemetery, engaging singers and caterers, among many other tasks that result in a successful well-attended event. The most important preparation was that of prayer. All the industry and diligence that we muster is woefully inadequate when one considers the possibilities of all that can go wrong in event planning.

The best blessing of that part of our trip was having Carl with me. I so enjoyed being with him in our apartment. We enjoyed just living life together and basking in the sunny peace of the completed mural. I think we had a little of God's own heart of satisfaction that we made it through—that this was a dream that was His and that He had allowed us to participate in. Now it was finished and we were glad. This sense of fulfillment touched me even as things got busier the closer we came to the dedication event. There is a scripture in the book of the Song of Solomon that says: *"Then was I in his eyes as one who found peace."* These words describe my sentiments nicely.

Dedication day arrived. It was 100 degrees Fahrenheit and I had a horrific headache. *"No!"* I cried inside. "Not today, not this special time; I want to feel good and be able to enjoy this day," was my plea to God. As we prepared and put the finishing touches on the details of the program, I watched as 120 people braved the heat to come to the dedication of the Jerusalem Wall of Life mural. I looked around and would have wept but the headache hindered me from tearful expression. I recognized almost every face that graced our day as the chairs filled to capacity. These were the people of Israel who connected with me during the six and a half years of the mural painting marathon. Each had contributed something of themselves to encourage me along the way. Many were now close friends whom I love dearly. There were Israelis, Arabs and Palestinians, Americans, Canadians, and many more ethnicities represented. All were comrades in the faith, who had at some point in the process left their gift of grace and urged me onward.

Among those who attended was the well-known Irene Levy, who was approaching 100 years of life. She came out to show her support and to join in the prayers of dedication. Irene witnessed Israel's War of Independence in her front row seat in Jerusalem. She has taught Hebrew to any who wanted to come learn for many years. What an honor for us to have her come. She said to me, "Oh I would not have missed this for anything."

Roger and Ellen were there and a key part of this program, to my delight. Roger gave a presentation and led the prayers of dedication. We had praise music from both Jewish and Arab believers. Carl and I, our team and the Alliance leaders laid our hands directly on the mural wall, anointing it with oil and surrendering it to the God of Israel for His kingdom purposes.

The event concluded as my dear friend sang an original song with her guitar. This song was about the amazing love of God, so fitting as we dedicated God's love story in pictures on the long wall. I shall always remember this special day.

"The 700 Club," from the Christian Broadcasting Network was also represented at the mural dedication. Chris Mitchell, CBN Bureau Chief, came to do a story about the mural which went out all across the globe. I felt embarrassed as I later watched the interview, knowing that literally millions had viewed it via satellite television. I was drenched from the sweat of that torrid day, my hair was kind of wild, plus I was in some realm of exuberance that defied my normal persona. I had to stake my claim that whatever happens with the mural, it is *not about me,* but rather something with eternal implications that was ordained from the beginning of time for *now*! So what if I looked weird? Now I can chuckle about it.

CHAPTER 47

One Last Poke

One week after the dedication of the mural, the Alliance and the mural team sponsored an open house event for our Israeli neighbors. We offered good food: American cuisine catered by Esther. Scot and I had traversed the neighborhood of the German Colony giving out small flyers in Hebrew and English, inviting all to come see the mural and have some good food. Without exception, people responded warmly to our invitation. Many shop keepers knew us now as familiar figures on Emek Rephaim St. They were all smiles with us.

The day of the open house event arrived. We had prepared a short program complete with speakers and Roy Kendall playing the keyboard. We had a turnout of approximately 50 people, including some surprises like Jan Willem and Ellen van der Hoeven, familiar figures in Israel, and the director of Masada Israel National Park whose father is buried in the cemetery. A sampling of our neighbors also attended. We had a healthy, happy mix of believers and non-believers.

When it was my turn to hold the mic, I gave a few insights into the complexity of my painting journey and spoke of my grateful heart for a transformed life. I also spoke of my Lithuanian heritage and lamented with tears their complicity in the Holocaust. Maybe my art could be a part of the healing of a nation, just maybe. As I was wrapping up my remarks and inviting people to join me in an 'artist's tour' of the mural, a force like a knock-out punch hit the back of my head. The pain it caused almost took my breath away. I could barely speak for a few moments. I recognized it immediately as a vicious attack from my adversary, Satan. I quickly concluded my remarks and grabbed Carl. *"Honey! Pray with me!"* I told him what had just happened and we prayed, taking authority against this demonic assault. The pain in the back of my head subsided but continued to cause misery.

Someone called to me to say that people were gathering for the tour I had promised. I defied the pain in my head and joined the group. With my usual animated delivery, I talked about the Creation, Abraham, and Moses and of course, Jesus, Yeshua. This mixed group of Jews, believing Jews and Christians smiled at me the entire time. I could feel them receiving my words. Nothing could diminish my joy. *"This is worth it all,"* I thought to myself as I told God's love story for all people.

The mural has taken on a life of its own. Thousands come in through the big black and gold iron gates of the Alliance International Cemetery and discover this is no ordinary cemetery. The peaceful presence, bright mural colors and pastoral feeling all add to a unique setting in a unique city. The local newspaper has the cemetery on its most unusual attractions in Jerusalem list. Trip Advisor touts it with a high rating for most interesting places in Israel. Photos have gone out over the Internet by people from all over the world who have entered the gates to see for themselves.

One Last Poke

You are invited to visit the mural website to see more.

www.jerusalemwalloflife.org

EPILOGUE

How does a Baby Boomer survive the mind boggling contradictions of the 60s that created the counter culture in the first place? The answer is simple but that does not mean it is easy; finding something so valuable that its worth cannot be measured in silver and gold, is to find the meaning of life. Simply put, it is worth everything. The daunting challenges I faced throughout my life have changed me. Something I could not do for myself was done for me when I said, "Yes." This broken hurting soul came to the only One who could do anything about it. He came with His comfort, forgiveness, and healing. However, He did not leave me like He found me, but bathed me in a love that put me in a war of clashing worlds. He empowered me to find my way and kept me safe the entire journey. Through all of this, I got to know Him quite well. What an adventure; what discoveries awaited me. Many will be so intoxicated with the ways of the cleverly disguised wisdom of the world, that they will not listen. *So my art cries.* My paintings, on a wall in an ancient city that witnessed the most extravagant love event of all time, cry out!

Again and again I return to the Alliance International Cemetery to receive our visitors from the neighborhood and the global neighborhood and give artist's tours. Telling the story of the Bible in the pictures on the mural wall is one of my greatest joys.

Life will most likely never be the 'same ole' life again

for me. As wrinkles make me *face* the reality of my years, I am determined not to let a little thing like age diminish my resolve to be jubilant. Reaching out to others has become my standard and it keeps me young. It is most rewarding to sit back in the quiet knowing that this Boomer has bloomed.

God lifts the poor and needy
from dust and ashes,
and he sets them with princes,
even the princes of His people.
He makes the barren woman to be a blessed
and a happy mother of children.
Psalm 113:7–9